POSTERS FOR PEACE

POSTERS FOR PEACE

VISUAL RHETORIC & CIVIC ACTION

THOMAS W. BENSON

The Pennsylvania
State University Press
University Park,
Pennsylvania

LIBRARY OF CONGRESS CATALOGING-IN-PUBLICATION DATA

Benson, Thomas W., author.
Posters for peace : visual rhetoric and civic action /
Thomas W. Benson.
    pages   cm
Summary: "A rhetorical history of Vietnam War
era posters produced at the University of California,
Berkeley, in the spring of 1970. Places the posters
in the contexts of the politics of the 1960s and the
history of political graphics"—Provided by publisher.
Includes bibliographical references and index.
ISBN 978-0-271-06586-1 (cloth : alk. paper)
1. Vietnam War, 1961–1975—Protest movements—
California—Berkeley—Posters. 2. United States—
Politics and government—1969–1974—Posters.
3. Political posters, American—California—Berkeley—
History—20th century. 4. University of California,
Berkeley—History—20th century. I. Title.

DS559.62.U6B46   2015
959.704'31—dc23
2014040914

The Pennsylvania State University Press is a member
of the Association of American University Presses.

It is the policy of The Pennsylvania State University
Press to use acid-free paper. Publications on uncoated
stock satisfy the minimum requirements of American
National Standard for Information Sciences—
Permanence of Paper for Printed Library Material,
ANSI Z39.48–1992.

Typeset by COGHILL COMPOSITION COMPANY

Printed and bound by SHERIDAN BOOKS

Composed in SCALA

Printed on ANTHEM MATTE

CONTENTS

PREFACE

Posters for Peace is a book about a collection of posters made and circulated on and about the campus of the University of California, Berkeley. In May 1970, as part of a national wave of protests against the Vietnam War, an invasion of Cambodia, and the killing of four students at Kent State University, groups of students at Berkeley produced and distributed a series of political posters. This book presents a rhetorical history and criticism, as well as a catalogue of a collection of some of the recovered posters, which are part of the Thomas W. Benson Political Protest Collection at the Penn State University Libraries.

Posters for Peace describes the rhetoric of those posters, using a historical and critical approach that places them in the circumstances of May 1970. It also employs comparative criticism to set the posters in the context of political discourse and political art more generally, and to consider them as works of visual rhetoric. The book ranges widely over the history and criticism of political debates and political graphics, especially regarding the 1960s and the war in Vietnam, with comparisons to international manifestations of visual and public rhetoric in more recent years. The general aim is to reconstruct the cultural and artistic resources that the artists drew on for inspiration, and to describe how viewers might have made sense of the Berkeley posters in 1970. I also offer a brief account of developments in rhetorical studies that were in part coincidental with the events of May 1970 and eventually gave rise to the subdiscipline of visual rhetoric that partly makes possible the analysis presented here. My own discipline, along with many others, was deeply influenced by the turmoil of the 1960s, as it developed new analytical resources in an attempt to fathom what was happening. I provide extensive notes and bibliography for those readers who want to pursue some of the topics that are treated here only briefly.

I was a witness to some of the events described in this history. I was a visiting professor of rhetoric at Berkeley in the 1969–70 academic year, where I gathered a large sample of the posters, which I kept for almost forty years. In 2008 I donated the posters and some related materials from the period to the library at Penn State University, where they form the basis of a continuing research archive, accompanied by an online digital collection.

ACKNOWLEDGMENTS

I am grateful to many colleagues and correspondents who provided crucial help in this project. James Quigel, head of the Historical Collections and Labor Archives at the Penn State University Libraries, worked with me in the transfer of the original posters to the Penn State collection, and supported the complex work of the Libraries in cataloguing, preserving, digitizing, and exhibiting the posters. Jim Quigel and Ellysa Stern Cahoy, Education Librarian, worked with others in the Libraries to post the collection online. To them and to others in the library who have supported this work, my thanks and admiration.

I am grateful for the remarkable and generous help of archivists and librarians to whom I have directed questions over the course of this project. At the University of California Archives at Bancroft Library on the Berkeley campus, David Kessler, Jason Miller, and others went out of their way to help a distant scholar; this help was further extended when I spent a week in the archives in February 2013. At a crucial point in my research into the archival holdings at Berkeley, poster historian Lincoln Cushing generously provided guidance on the location of the key collection. At the University of British Columbia, Vancouver, Christopher Hives and Katherine Kalsbeek offered help when it was needed. I have also been assisted by archivists and others at the US National Archives and Records Administration, the Imperial War Museum (United Kingdom), and the Bibliothèque nationale de France; Jon Fletcher at the Richard Nixon Presidential Library; and Geoffrey D. Swindells of the Northwestern University Library.

I am grateful to colleagues who responded to early versions of this work with generosity and good questions. Diane Hope, late Kern Professor of Communication emerita at the Rochester Institute of Technology, invited me to present a keynote lecture on the Berkeley posters in April 2008 at a conference on visual communication that she organized in Rochester. She also provided encouragement, as did other scholars of visual rhetoric who attended the lecture. That lecture is an early version of what became this book. Later versions of the analysis were presented as a gallery talk in the Paterno Library at Penn State University, in November 2011, at the invitation of, and with the support of, Jim Quigel and Ellysa Cahoy, and at a colloquium of the Department of Communication Arts and Sciences at Penn State. My thanks to them and to colleagues at both occasions, who asked questions and offered suggested lines of analysis that have been helpful.

I thank my colleagues and students at Penn State University, who are a continuing source of inspiration and support. Stephen Browne, Rosa Eberly, Cara Finnegan, John Gastil, Kevin Hagopian, David Calandra, Brian Curran, Philip Rogers, Susan Squier, and Brian Snee offered encouragement and useful questions. Phil Rogers, discerning reader and old friend, read the entire manuscript and offered many valuable suggestions. The ongoing support of the College of the Liberal Arts and of the faculty and students of the Department of Communication Arts and Sciences has been generous and unstinting. The Penn State University endowment for the Edwin Erle Sparks Professor of Rhetoric has made possible some research time and indispensable support for travel to archives and acquisition of research materials, and a sabbatical leave made possible the time needed to complete the research and writing.

Kendra Boileau, editor in chief of the Penn State University Press, gave me early encouragement and ongoing support as my editor for the project, and many others at Penn State University Press have been helpful along the way. Robert Turchick, editorial assistant, assisted with the acquisition of images and other tasks; my copyeditor was S. Scott Rohrer. Patrick Alexander, director, offered perspective and encouragement.

My family has given support, suggestions, and love—daughters Daisy and Sarah Benson; granddaughter Lucia Benson-Ruth; son-in-law Richard Ruth and daughter-in-law Hannah Peacock. My wife of more than fifty years, Margaret Sandelin Benson, has encouraged me at every stage, all these years.

POSTERS FOR PEACE

POSTERS FOR PEACE

Visual Rhetoric and Civic Action

This book is an account of the visual rhetoric of a collection of peace posters created in Berkeley, California, in 1970, and of the circumstances in which they were brought into being and given meaning. The posters themselves were a small but telling part of an energetic and diverse movement by American college students in the 1960s and early 1970s against war and racism. Student activism in the United States in the 1960s was part of a loosely connected worldwide movement that took on different forms—most memorably, perhaps, in 1968. The events of May 1970 brought a terrible climax to a long period of confusion and turmoil.

Posters for Peace begins with an extended essay on the rhetorical history of the posters and their immediate and longer-term historical context. It offers close readings of the posters from a rhetorical perspective, with comparisons to other visual examples where appropriate, and with annotations to explain some of the posters' multiple cultural meanings. The rhetorical approach attempted here regards the posters as addressed to viewers—in this case, by unknown artists to unspecified audiences—and it explores their antecedents, contexts, and forms. Through close reading and comparative analysis, this approach attempts to recover and reimagine the potential experiences invited by the posters as rhetoric. The second section of the book presents a gallery of the Berkeley posters in the Protest Posters Collection at the Penn State University Libraries. The posters themselves are now owned by the Historical Collections and Labor Archives in the

FIGURE 1   "Peace Now." Berkeley, California, 1970.
Thomas W. Benson Political Protest Collection,
Historical Collections and Labor Archives, Eberly
Family Special Collections Library, University
Libraries, The Pennsylvania State University.

Eberly Family Special Collections Library. A condition of their gift to Penn State was that they should be freely available for nonprofit educational uses. They are also available online at the library and at the Flickr Creative Commons.[1]

The close-reading approach is an attempt to recover how the posters might have looked in 1970. This is partly an exercise in recovery—recovery of the meanings that might have been invited by and achieved by these posters in 1970—but also reflects an understanding that the posters are of interest as part of the continuing conversation of American culture. Recovering the meanings that might have been circulating in 1970 is not simply an exercise in taxidermy, the recovery of an inert and bygone moment. Our own historical and political context may distort our capacity to recover the posters' rhetoric as it existed in 1970. And yet, a reader of this book might very well want to look at these posters precisely to make use of them. Understanding something more about them as part of a context will perhaps make that recovery more useful.

The close reading of visual rhetoric begins by attending to the primary, manifest verbal and visual content, as well as the primary stylistic features—color, form, line, and so on. *Comparative, inventional,* and *audience* perspectives guide the analysis. A comparative approach, when undertaken from a rhetorical perspective, as in this study, has multiple, overlapping dimensions. The posters' direct appeal stems from their location within the larger rhetorical currents of the time—both the "moment" of May 1970 and the broader political and cultural rhetorics of the long 1960s. A comparative approach to the posters as *visual* rhetoric seeks to invite the reader to view the posters in context and in contrast to earlier and later visual rhetorics that may or may not have been accessible to the artists and audiences of the posters in 1970; such an approach helps us to see what contemporaries probably took for granted, things seen but not explicitly noticed by artists and audiences in 1970. A study of the pre-1970 history of the poster and of political graphics may provide clues into what may be called the *inventional rhetoric* of the posters—that is, the resources, traditions, and rhetorical iconographies that the poster artists may have consulted, directly or indirectly, as they created the images considered here. A parallel comparative approach attempts to reconstruct what might be called the *rhetoric of reception,* which takes into account the resources of those who viewed and perhaps recirculated the posters in 1970. These three comparative approaches—of the poster artist, of the 1970 poster viewer, and of the reader who comes upon the posters decades later and seeks to recover them for the present—are not entirely exclusive, but they are conceptually different. In any case, the close readings and the comparisons are undertaken from a rhetorical perspective—this study seeks to understand the posters not primarily as part of the history of art but as works of visual rhetoric and civic persuasion.

The study of rhetoric was itself at a transformative moment in 1970, and that transformation is part of the story I attempt to tell in these pages. In May 1970, the month these posters were circulating in Berkeley, a group of scholars came together in the National Developmental Project in Rhetoric. The 1960s campus politics of civil liberties, civil rights, and peace helped to prompt a redirection and renewal of rhetorical studies; those changes in rhetorical studies, especially the development of studies in visual rhetoric, provide some of the grounding of the present study, and they may be seen as one example of how the 1960s prompted transformations in disciplines across the humanities and social sciences.

In 1970 some art historians would have argued that these posters were mere illustration or graphic design, but not art. Similarly, some rhetorical scholars would have argued that posters were not rhetoric in the full sense of the term—some scholars and gatekeepers saw "rhetoric" as being limited to persuasive verbal discourse, or even more narrowly to public oratory. In this study, I do not ask whether the posters are art or rhetoric (or even whether they are neither). Instead, I assume they are at least in some sense both, and I inquire into how they played their part in the politics of 1970. "Posters," writes Jeffrey T. Schnapp, "provide a literal, material bridge between the new public sphere constituted by mass communications and the public spaces that become the sites of modern politics as street theater."[2] For decades, posters had been employed as agencies of state propaganda and popular protest. In *The Power of the Poster*, Margaret Timmers notes, "By its nature, the poster has the ability to seize the immediate attention of the viewer, and then to retain it for what is usually a brief but intense period. During that span of attention, it can provoke and motivate its audience—it can make the viewer gasp, laugh, reflect, question, assent, protest, recoil, or otherwise react. This is part of the process by which the message is conveyed and, in successful cases, ultimately acted upon. At its most effective, the poster is a dynamic force for change."[3] So familiar are we with the poster as a rhetorical object that when we notice a poster we instantly understand that it is asking something of us—or of someone. Posters, as they exist in our vernacular cultural experience, are fundamentally rhetorical. In Berkeley, California, in May 1970, student protesters used posters to mobilize citizens for continuing opposition to the Vietnam War in the name of enduring American ideals.

A Time to Kill, and a Time to Heal

On the evening of April 30, 1970, President Richard Nixon addressed the country on national television, announcing that US forces were entering Cambodia—an incursion that would expand the Vietnam War (see fig. 2). He said, in part,

> Tonight, American and South Vietnamese units will attack the headquarters for the entire Communist military operation in South Vietnam. This key control center has been occupied by the North Vietnamese and Vietcong for five years in blatant violation of Cambodia's neutrality.
>
> This is not an invasion of Cambodia. The areas in which these attacks will be launched are completely occupied and controlled by North Vietnamese forces. Our purpose is not to occupy the areas. Once enemy forces are driven out of these sanctuaries, and once their military supplies are destroyed, we will withdraw.

Nixon acknowledged that the American people wanted to see an end to the war, but he appealed for support for an invasion that he described as part of a plan that would allow the United States to withdraw from Vietnam. He issued a warning to those people, especially student radicals, opposing his program: "My fellow Americans, we live in an age of anarchy, both abroad and at home. We see mindless attacks on all the great institutions which have been created by free civilizations in the last 500 years. Even here in the United States, great universities are being systematically destroyed."[4] Despite Nixon's attempt to portray the Cambodian adventure as merely an "incursion" by the armed forces of South Vietnam, the growing opposition to the president's Vietnam policies in Congress and among the press strongly denounced the action as an illegal US invasion of Cambodia.[5]

Senator Charles Goodell, a Republican from New York who had been appointed to fill the unexpired term of the assassinated Robert F. Kennedy in 1968, introduced a resolution of impeachment. Two days after Nixon's speech, James Reston wrote in the *New York Times* that "it is a thunderingly silly argument to suggest [as Nixon had] that wiping out the enemy's bases in Cambodia will get to 'the heart of the trouble.'" Reston argued that "as a television show and a political exercise it [the speech] may have been effective, but as a serious Presidential presentation of the brutal facts of a tragic and dangerous problem of world politics, it was ridiculous."[6]

FIGURE 2   Richard Nixon, Cambodia Address,
April 30, 1970. Photograph by Jack E. Kightlinger.
White House Photo Office, WHPO 3448–21A.
Courtesy Richard Nixon Library, National Archives
and Records Administration.

By 1970 student opposition to the war had become widespread, and the Cambodian invasion stimulated protests across the country. In some cases, ROTC buildings on campuses were destroyed, although it was not always clear whether
students were responsible.[7] Student leaders called for a national student strike
against the war. It is difficult now to recall how unsteady the United States seemed
to be in those days. Watergate, with all of its dislocations, was still ahead, but in less
than ten years America had witnessed the murders of President John F. Kennedy
and his brother, Robert, and African American leaders Malcolm X, Medgar Evers,
and Martin Luther King Jr. Police attacked dissidents in Chicago for the 1968 Democratic National Convention in what official reports later called a police riot, and
rioters torched America's inner cities. Analysts wrote of "student unrest" and "civil
disturbances," and wondered whether history itself was broken.

President Nixon and other national politicians stoked resentment against the
students. On May 1, the day after his Cambodia address, Nixon visited the Pentagon

for a military briefing and stopped to speak with a group of civilian employees. A woman in the group told Nixon, "I loved your speech. It made me proud to be an American." A *New York Times* reporter recounts the incident:

> Smiling and obviously pleased, Mr. Nixon stopped and told how he had been thinking, as he wrote his speech, about "those kids out there [in Vietnam]."
> "I have seen them. They are the greatest," he said. Then he contrasted them with antiwar activists on university campuses. According to a White House text of his remarks, he said:
> "You see these bums, you know, blowing up the campuses. Listen, the boys that are on the college campuses today are the luckiest people in the world, going to the greatest universities, and here they are burning up the books, storming around about this issue. You name it. Get rid of the war there will be another one."

The *Times* reporter wrote, "The President's use of the term 'bums' to refer to student radicals was the strongest language he has used publicly on the subject of campus violence, although he has been known to employ such terms in private."[8]

On May 2, the Army ROTC building at Kent State University in Ohio was burned down during a student antiwar demonstration. The circumstances were suspicious enough that serious observers speculated the fire might have been part of a scenario of provocation by police or other government agents.[9] On Sunday, May 3, Ohio governor James Rhodes, a Republican who was trailing in his Senate primary campaign, took advantage of the situation to visit Kent State, where he vowed to keep the university open despite the advice of others that closing it for a time would allow things to calm down. Rhodes held a news conference, warning,

> The scene here that the city of Kent is facing is probably the most vicious form of campus-oriented violence yet perpetrated by dissident groups and their allies in the State of Ohio. . . . We're going to use every weapon of law enforcement agencies of Ohio to drive them out of Kent. . . . They're worse than the brownshirts and the Communist element and also the night riders and the vigilantes. They're the worst type of people that we harbor in America. . . . We are going to eradicate the problem, we're not going to treat the symptoms.[10]

Asked by reporters what the governor's remarks meant for the National Guard, "General Del Corso clarified it for the newsmen. 'As the Ohio law says,' the general pointed out, 'use any force that's necessary even to the point of shooting. We don't want to get into that, but the law says we can if necessary.'"[11]

The next day they did. After chasing students, including many who were simply walking to class, across the Kent State campus, the National Guard slashed several students with bayonets and later fired at students who presented no immediate threat to the Guard or others. Four students were killed. Nine were wounded by gunfire.

The events at Kent State intensified campus protests across the nation. After Nixon's Cambodia speech, many university presidents shut down their campuses for short periods or for the rest of the academic year—Columbia University was closed from May 2, and some other campuses followed after Kent State. Student strikes and demonstrations spread rapidly.

Nixon supported the National Guard while implicitly disclaiming responsibility for the massacre. At the regular White House news briefing on May 4, press secretary Ronald Ziegler read a statement from the president: "This should remind us all once again that when dissent turns to violence, it invites tragedy. It is my hope that this tragic and unfortunate incident will strengthen the determination of all the Nation's campuses—administration, faculty, and students alike—to stand firmly for the right which exists in this country of peaceful dissent and just as strongly against the resort to violence as a means of such expression."[12] Nixon's rhetoric in this statement is peculiar—the only active agents to whom he alludes are "administration, faculty, and students," who appear to be responsible for inviting tragedy. The National Guard and Nixon himself disappear into the passive voice. But the president also professed his good intentions.

In New York City on May 8, construction workers using crowbars, other tools, and hard hats attacked an antiwar rally on Wall Street held in honor of the Kent State victims. Seventy people were injured. The mayhem spread to City Hall, where an American flag flew at half staff to commemorate the Kent State students: the construction workers demanded that it be raised to full staff. Other rioters attacked the nearby Trinity Episcopal Church, tearing down its flag and a Red Cross banner.[13] It was rhetorically convenient for the Nixon administration and its supporters to depict resistance to the Vietnam War as limited to radical, privileged college students, and this depiction has survived in collective memory. And yet many working-class Americans opposed the war, and the draft, and resistance to the war could be found in all ranks of society and in the military.[14]

At his evening news conference on May 8, President Nixon was asked repeatedly about student dissent and his administration's reaction to it. Herbert Kaplow
of NBC News questioned the president about what he thought the students were
trying to say. Nixon replied, "They are trying to say they want peace. They are trying
to say they want to stop the killing. They are trying to say that they want to end the
draft. They are trying to say that we ought to get out of Vietnam. I agree with everything that they are trying to accomplish."[15] At five o'clock the next morning, President Nixon, accompanied by his valet, Manolo Sanchez, traveled to the Lincoln
Memorial for an unplanned predawn conversation with fifty or so students who
were in town for antiwar protests. In his *Vietnam: A History*, Stanley Karnow wrote
that Nixon "treated them to a clumsy and condescending monologue, which he
made public in an awkward attempt to display his benevolence."[16] Soon afterward,
in actions that led directly to Watergate and the fall of his presidency, Nixon
"ordered the formation of a covert team headed by Tom Huston, a former Army
intelligence specialist, to improve the surveillance of domestic critics. During later
investigations into Nixon's alleged violations of the law, Senator Sam Ervin of North
Carolina called the Huston project evidence of a 'Gestapo mentality,' and Huston
himself warned Nixon that the internal espionage was illicit."[17]

Shortly after midnight on May 15, 1970, on the campus of Jackson State University in Jackson, Mississippi, city and state police fired at a group of protesting students. Two students, one from Jackson State and the other a local high school
student, were killed; twelve others were struck by gunfire. President Nixon
expressed his regrets and continued his public campaign for support of his war
policies. At the end of May, he appeared at a Billy Graham revival for a photo oppor-
tunity. Meanwhile, student protests continued around the country.

At the Berkeley campus of the University of California, political protest had
been intense since the day after Nixon's Cambodia speech. Berkeley had been the
scene of student political activity since at least 1958, when some student leaders
founded SLATE, a loose confederation of progressive students, both graduate and
undergraduate, to run as a united ticket in student-government elections. The
administration had responded by removing graduate students from the student-
government elections and by taking other actions to impede student political
action. In 1960, the House Un-American Activities Committee held hearings at
City Hall in San Francisco. Students from around the Bay Area picketed the hearings to protest that the committee was an enemy of civil liberties. Police with fire
hoses attacked them and dragged them down the long flight of marble steps at the
center of the City Hall rotunda, hauling the protesters away in paddy wagons.

As the civil rights movement gained momentum, especially after the sit-ins of 1960, the Freedom Rides of 1961, and voter registration campaigns in Mississippi, Berkeley students circulated information and collected money on campus and at the traditional cluster of tables at the southern entrance of the university at the intersection of Telegraph and Bancroft. The university responded by declaring new rules prohibiting any campus political activity about anything other than purely university business. These restrictions gave rise to the Free Speech Movement at Berkeley, which played out over the academic year of 1964–65. On October 1, 1964, a former graduate student who was sitting at the CORE table was arrested. The police car was immediately surrounded by hundreds of students. Over the next several days, support for the students grew. These were the demonstrations that made Mario Savio famous nationally.[18]

In April 1969 a loose coalition of Berkeley residents and students declared the inauguration of what they called People's Park on a vacant lot that the university had designated for eventual development but which was sitting unused just a short walk south of the university. The People's Park movement quickly drew the enthusiasm of a diverse group of students, progressives, hippies, and local community activists. The university responded that they had no business being on the site, but then agreed that it would not evict them from the park without further negotiations. At this point, Ronald Reagan, who had been elected governor in 1966 in a campaign partly directed against the Berkeley campus, intervened.

Reagan sent the National Guard—almost 3,000 troops—and a large group of sheriff's deputies—nearly 800—into Berkeley, where, in May 1969, the deputies shot and killed Berkeley student James Rector, an innocent bystander, with a volley of buckshot. Today a mural at the corner of Haste Street and Telegraph Avenue in Berkeley depicts the moment just after Rector was shot (see fig. 3); this section of the mural is based on a photograph taken on the scene by Kathryn Bigelow that was widely circulated at the time. The first publication of the Bigelow photograph of the dying James Rector appears to have been in the *Berkeley Barb*, an underground newspaper, in its May 23–29 issue, where it features in a group of photographs that also show armed and uniformed men on the street pointing their weapons at the rooftops.[19] The Bigelow photograph does not include the men who were aiming shotguns at the rooftop.[20] Others were wounded by buckshot and tear gas that day and in the weeks of the occupation.

The long history of these events created a student movement of considerable experience and commitment. It also created a long history of distrust between the university administration and the governor's office, on the one hand, and the

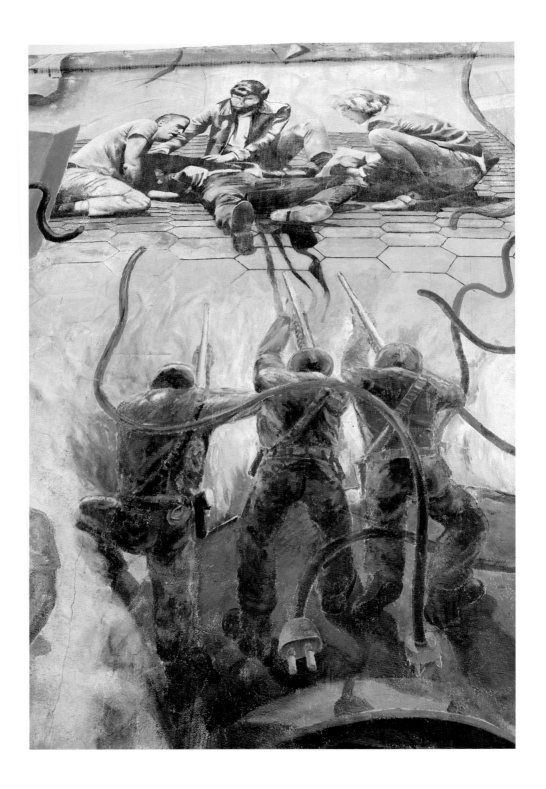

student leaders and those who sympathized with them on the other, with the Berkeley faculty distributed across the spectrum of opinion and in the middle. The experience of a campus community, and especially of its students, is in many ways discontinuous, because the students are on campus for only a few years. Not all of the history that it is possible to summarize now would have been entirely accessible to the student body. But this truism can work both ways. The indignation and the organizational skills that had repeatedly sparked into being in the decade before May 1970, both over broad issues such as race and war and over the more local frictions between administrators and students, were partly carried off campus with each graduating class. On the other hand, Berkeley gained a reputation as a center of campus activism, which attracted new recruits and allowed the creation of a large core of committed and experienced organizers. The intensity and visibility of the 1960s protest movement in Berkeley, and the continuing publication of movement news and history in local and national sources, kept the history alive and vivid.

As the new academic year of 1969–70 began, just months after the People's Park attacks, political activity was in daily evidence on campus, especially antiwar appeals, but the tone was muted for the most part, and politics and the war were clearly not the main interests of most students. Yet the war and the state did intrude.

On November 12, 1969, Seymour Hersh of the *St. Louis Post-Dispatch* broke the story of the My Lai massacre, which had taken place in March 1968. At the village of My Lai, some 350 to 500 innocents, mostly women, children, and old men, had been killed by US troops: many of the victims were lined up at a ditch and executed. News of My Lai left faculty and students shaken and shocked.[21]

Governor Reagan continued to campaign against the students. In early fall 1969, he announced plans for a 25 percent budget cut for the University of California. In the spring, he intensified his anti-university campaign. As the story is told by Reagan biographer Lou Cannon, three weeks before President Nixon's Cambodian invasion was announced, Governor Reagan made a remark that seemed consistent with his actions toward Berkeley. "On April 7, 1970, addressing the California Council of Growers at Yosemite, Reagan was asked about the on-campus tactics of the New Left. 'If it takes a bloodbath, let's get it over with,' Reagan responded. 'No more appeasement.'"[22] Reagan's remarks were quoted in a widely circulated underground newspaper, the *Berkeley Tribe*.[23]

FIGURE 3   James Rector mural (detail). Haste
Street and Telegraph Avenue, Berkeley, California.
Photograph by the author, 2013.

On the Berkeley campus in the days after President Nixon's Cambodia speech, having heard Reagan's threatening words and others like them, students tried to thread their way safely to class through roving bands of aggressive deputies and sought to avoid clouds of tear gas, fired sometimes from grenade launchers, other times from hovering helicopters: it seemed as if the governor's office was at war with the university. This experience on the campus went on, day after day, and with special intensity after Nixon's Cambodia speech.

At Berkeley and many other universities and colleges, demonstrations and strikes were called. When, after the Kent State killings on May 4, several college presidents shut down their institutions for the rest of the academic year, students at Berkeley, instead of declaring a boycott or simply going home, adopted the slogan "On Strike—Keep It Open." They in effect declared a campus-wide teach-in, asserting and identifying with the ongoing value of the university's core educational mission. Student and faculty activity persisted even after Governor Reagan ordered the campus shut down for the remainder of the week after Kent State.[24] Some classes were canceled, and some students went home. Other classes continued to meet, in some cases revising their agendas to address the current emergency. At least one class was canceled when the teacher and students arrived to find that a tear gas grenade had been thrown through a closed window into the classroom shortly before. There were daily rallies in Sproul Plaza.

Be Young and Shut Up

Some yards east of Sproul Plaza and up the hill is Wurster Hall, home of the College of Environmental Design. Early in May, students there began to create and freely distribute antiwar posters. The Berkeley poster project may have been inspired in part by the posters produced by art students in Paris in May 1968— who were in turn, perhaps, indirectly inspired by the Berkeley protests of the early 1960s. The Paris students had created what they called the Atelier Populaire, producing a series of freely distributed posters. The Atelier Populaire was the name given to themselves by a group of Parisian students at the École des Beaux-Arts. On May 8, 1968, the École des Beaux-Arts went on strike. A series of massive demonstrations was called, involving both workers and students, in Paris and around the country. According to an account by striking students, on May 14 a "provisional strike committee informs the Administrative Council of the Ecole des Beaux-Arts that the students are taking possession of the premises."[25] This passage first appears, in French, in a small book published in Paris in 1969. In *Posters from the Revolution, Paris, May, 1968*, a translated version appeared that included, in large format, color prints of some of the posters. Records of the Bancroft Library at the University of California, Berkeley, indicate that the library owns two copies of the 1969 English version, and that one of them is in the library of the College of Environmental Design, where the Berkeley posters were produced. If the book was there in 1970 (and there is every reason to suppose that it was), then it would have been available as a resource for Berkeley faculty and students involved in the Berkeley poster project.

Other lines of apparent or potential connection link the Berkeley posters with the Paris of May 1968. A famous Paris poster from that month shows Adolf Hitler holding a mask of Charles de Gaulle (see fig. 4).[26] A corresponding Berkeley poster

FIGURE 4   [Hitler tenant à la main le masque de de Gaulle (Hitler holding in his hand the mask of de Gaulle)]. Atelier Populaire, May 1968. Bibliothèque nationale de France.

of May 1970 shows Hitler holding a mask of Richard Nixon (plate 16). Since the
de Gaulle–Hitler poster does not appear in the 1968 Paris book *Atelier Populaire* or
in *Posters from the Revolution*, there must have been several routes of influence
between Berkeley and Paris. The behind-the-mask iconology has a long history. In
the collection of the Imperial War Museum in the United Kingdom is a German
World War I poster, "Hinter der Maske," showing a lean, angry, red-faced man
holding up a smiling, round-faced, white mask—a spy pretending to be a friendly
burgher.[27] The theme has a still longer history in the wolf-in-sheep's-clothing fable,
which appears in the New Testament ("Beware of false prophets, which come to
you in sheep's clothing, but inwardly they are ravening wolves" [Matthew 7:15]), and
in a tale that became associated with an Aesop fable about a wolf, raised among
sheep dogs, that reverted to type.

The Paris protests arose most immediately from brutal police attacks on demon-
strating students, creating a widespread student movement that was joined by factory workers and other labor groups. A key theme in Paris, as in the Berkeley
demonstrations of 1970, was to protest the suppression of free speech, as in the
poster "Sois jeune et tais toi" (see fig. 5), in which a silhouette of de Gaulle holds his
hand over the mouth of a student and admonishes him, "Be young and shut up."

The Paris posters celebrated the solidarity of the students and striking factory
workers, mocked state-owned national television as a propaganda apparatus,
depicted de Gaulle as a monarch, and scorned an emergency election as a mere
plebiscite, after which de Gaulle would simply resume his rule.[28] Several posters
asserted that the struggle would continue—a slogan that still echoes in European
political graffiti decades later. The Vietnam War had less salience in Paris than in
the United States in 1968, but it was a theme of some posters and, according to
participants, partly motivated their objection to state authority.

French thought and French student politics probably had some influence on
developments in the United States, but this influence was mostly indirect and cultural. The works of existentialists Jean-Paul Sartre and Albert Camus had been
widely read in American colleges for years. Student and counterculture magazines
carried news of the New Left and its thought. French cultural theory that had
informed Paris '68—for example, the Situationist International theories of Guy
Debord—was in circulation in the United States from the mid-1960s, although it
was not widely known.[29] Debord's *La société du spectacle* was published in Paris in
1967; the first English translation appeared in 1970. Debord argued that all contemporary experience occurs as spectacle, in which the dominant order presents
itself everywhere—public and private, work and leisure—as normal: "The specta-

FIGURE 5   "Sois jeune et tais toi" (Be young and
shut up). Atelier Populaire, May 1968. Bibliothèque
nationale de France.

cle is the existing order's uninterrupted discourse about itself, its laudatory monologue. It is the self-portrait of power in the epoch of its totalitarian management of
the conditions of existence."[30] American radicals were also familiar with British
radical thought. The *New Left Review* had begun publication in 1960, in London,
circulating New Left thinking internationally.

In the United States, the New Left was perhaps most clearly identified with Students for a Democratic Society, although liberal, radical, and countercultural thought was fragmented and widespread in and beyond SDS. Berkeley, a center of political action through the decade, was not reducible to SDS, according to contemporary and later accounts. The SDS itself went through rapid change throughout the period. In addition to the diverse political atmosphere in and accessible to Berkeley, the musical and cultural revolutions of the 1960s were everywhere visible and audible, with the nearby, iconic Haight-Ashbury counterculture and the strong Bay Area presence of rock concerts and psychedelic art. And yet with all the sources that the Berkeley graphic artists had available to them, the overriding tone in May 1970 seems to appeal to fundamentally liberal and democratic values—though of course this might be because as a rhetorical matter the discourse was addressed and not simply expressed. By May 1970, Students for a Democratic Society had become radicalized to the threshold of self-destruction, although SDS leaders were still active at Berkeley. In fact, Tom Hayden, who had helped found SDS and who was the author of its founding manifesto, *The Port Huron Statement*, addressed an audience at the outdoor theater on campus in May 1970.[31]

The Paris posters, and the entire Paris '68 movement, were on the whole much more militant than the Berkeley posters.[32] The Paris posters denounced President de Gaulle and the French police, whose brutal suppression of peaceful demonstrations at the Sorbonne and among workers led to waves of protest and the near destruction of the government itself (see fig. 6). At one point, in the face of continued demonstrations and a general strike in all segments of the economy, and fearing that his government could collapse within forty-eight hours, de Gaulle secretly left Paris to consult with a French general stationed in Germany to bargain for army support. The student posters in Paris celebrated a unity and common interest between workers and students in a way that never applied in the United States, where the Nixon administration retained the support of a large segment of the white working class. But for all its militancy, the poster campaign of the Atelier Populaire was deliberately not sectarian. In 2012, William Bostwick interviewed Philippe Vermés, one of the Atelier Populaire artists, on the occasion of the publication of a new book on the Paris posters. Vermés recalls that "when we were occupying the Beaux-Arts, we'd have a meeting every night at 7 P.M. to decide on a slogan. We said, We have to not be Trotskyites, Situationists, anarchists. We have to get the right slogan that hits people the strongest. We'd vote. . . . One time, we made a flag, blue, white, and red. And the red overlapped the other colors, and—no, no, no, we

FIGURE 6 "La beauté est dans la rue" (Beauty is in the street). Atelier Populaire. Bibliothèque nationale de France.

said. Because maybe it's a Communist red. Everyone had to put their ideologies behind them."[33]

The Paris posters were almost certainly known to at least some of the Berkeley artists. The first published versions, together with an account of how they were created, in *Atelier Populaire: Présenté par lui-meme* (Paris, 1968) were succeeded the next year by a large-format English translation copublished by Dobson Books in London and Bobbs-Merrill in Indianapolis as *Posters from the Revolution, Paris, May, 1968: Texts and Posters* (1969). On the copyright page of both books, here using the English version of 1969, is this statement:

> To the reader:
> The posters reproduced by the Atelier Populaire are weapons in the service of the struggle and are an inseparable part of it.

Their rightful place is in the centres of conflict, that is to say in the streets and on the walls of the factories. To use them for decorative purposes, to display them in bourgeois places of culture or to consider them as objects of aesthetic interest is to impair both their function and their effect. This is why the Atelier Populaire has always refused to put them on sale.

Even to keep them as historical evidence of a certain stage of the struggle is a betrayal, for the struggle itself is of such primary importance that the position of an "outside" observer is a fiction which inevitably plays into the hands of the ruling class.

That is why this book should not be taken as the final outcome of an experience, but as an inducement for finding, through contact with the masses, new levels of action both on the cultural and the political plane.[34]

The Atelier Populaire posters may themselves have been inspired by posters from Berkeley in the mid-1960s, when artists were experimenting with silk screen and photo-offset techniques for creating psychedelic poster art and political protest posters. John Barnicoat, author of a standard history of the poster, in an article in *Grove Art Online*, traces Berkeley psychedelic posters of 1965 back to the late nineteenth century. Rather than suggesting that the earlier Berkeley posters directly influenced the Atelier Populaire posters of 1968, Barnicoat appears to argue that similar political and material circumstances were the occasion of a parallel movement.

The events of May 1968 in Paris also produced posters that were evidence of a new generation asserting itself. A more serious political aim provided the background to the crude, screen-printed images generated by the Atelier Populaire, established in May 1968. Here cooperation between amateur and professional talent resulted in a series of small posters such as the caricature of General de Gaulle in *La Chienlit—c'est lui* (1968; Paris, Lesley Hamilton priv. col.), which restored the poster to its original function as a fly-posted handbill. Such had been the poster's development as a sophisticated vehicle, expensive to produce and dependent on the support of the social and business establishments and their technical resources, that when such support was removed, poster design reverted to its origin as a hand-printed sheet. Inevitably, the situation affected both image and form, and helped restore the poster to its original function as a "noisy" street announcement.[35]

Historian Michael Seidman notes that the Paris posters were "the most striking and enduring cultural legacy" of May 1968.[36] He argues that the practical effects of May 1968 in Paris were limited, but that they have achieved a place in collective memory, perhaps in large part because of the afterlife of the posters, and have "become a symbol of a youthful, renewed, and freer France."[37] Marc Rohan, who as a student participated in the Paris demonstrations, recalls that the posters and graffiti "covered the walls" and that they "were to become the most imaginative art form of the period."[38]

In an oral history interview, artist Rupert Garcia testifies to a direct link between the Atelier Populaire and posters in the Bay Area. Garcia, then an art student at San Francisco State, recalls that in late 1968 or early 1969,

> well, in the art department we did eventually respond, in terms of faculty. . . . We had a big meeting of art students and faculty about how to address the campus strike. And one faculty—I guess, a faculty from England, who had just come back from visiting France and Paris—mentioned to us what he saw some students doing there—which was to make posters. And so we— some faculty and students—organized a poster brigade. And we used Dennis Beall's print studios and his instruction on how to do silk screen and so we learned this technique, like on-the-job training. There was no course, no class. And I was a liaison between the art department and the other members of the Third World Liberation Front organizations. I would go talk to them and come back, and this kind of thing. And so we began to make posters dealing with the issues—issues from racism to better education to police brutality, anti-war, and much more. I mean, all the issues that were being addressed at that time made for a heady experience. Many of those issues were being dealt with in our poster brigade. And the posters were used in the demonstrations on campus, and some were used outside of campus, and some were sold to raise money to get people out on bail, people who had been arrested. And it was going very well. We had really wonderful teamwork.[39]

Peace Is Patriotic

In Berkeley itself, the posters from 1970 were clearly a continuation of the local posters from the mid-1960s and earlier.[40] In January 1966, Bill Graham began organizing rock music dance concerts at the Fillmore Auditorium in San Francisco, and he hired artists to create posters advertising the events. The posters spread throughout the Bay Area and attracted international attention. The posters, by a variety of artists, suggested both the psychedelic subculture centered in San Francisco and the rock music that was their direct subject. Walter Medeiros, a historian of the posters, describes them as handmade and hand-lettered, with rich decorative patterns, "abstract, undulating, stretched or warped," with bright colors in unusual combinations, and with images that are "sensual, bizarre or beautiful, philosophical or metaphysical."[41] The handmade posters were then commercially printed in large numbers and distributed throughout the Bay Area, a congenial place for the circulation and viewing of posters. Graham later recalled,

> I was possessed. I'd go out there all speeded up on my scooter with my Army pack. . . . I would stick a big pile of posters in there with my industrial stapler. And in my coat, my fiberglass 3M tape, so I could put posters up on steel or concrete, not just wood. I would leave the city at four in the morning and go up to Berkeley . . . [and] when people woke up in the morning, full. Every wall. I knew then that the posters were hitting home, because as I went back down the block, I would see people taking them off the wall for their own.[42]

The dance concert posters and the Berkeley peace posters also shared a common space that was, it turned out, suited to the display of posters and directed to a public familiar with street poster art. In a 1974 article, Marc Treib described how the mild weather in Berkeley drew people onto the streets, especially in the Telegraph Avenue area just south of campus at Sproul Plaza. After earlier demonstrators had broken storefront windows along Telegraph, owners replaced glass with plywood or with windowless walls, and these surfaces became prime locations for posters, especially "cheap photocopy and offset lithography . . . in near standard format. The machines limit the message size to 8" by 11" or 8½" by 14", usually one color." The posters were stapled or taped to telephone poles, walls, and kiosks, becoming a "town crier, the information source."[43] Alton Kelley, one of the dance concert poster artists, observed later that Berkeley and San Francisco were ideal physical settings for the concert posters, a setting that was much the same in May 1970 when the Berkeley peace posters were in circulation. Kelley recalls, "The posters wouldn't have worked in any other city. New York's too big, and nobody walks in L.A. So what you had in San Francisco was the right combination of people walking around the streets and timing. Everything that was happening in the culture came together—at least for a while."[44]

The dance concert posters were not "political" in the same way that the peace posters were. In his dissertation on the psychedelic rock concert posters, Kevin Moist nevertheless identifies what he calls a "form of subcultural visionary rhetoric." Moist writes that in Haight-Ashbury, the core of the psychedelic culture, "during the mid-to-late 1960s we find nary a protest nor political demonstration of any kind."[45] Moist argues that the Haight subculture did have a politics, but that hippie politics refused what it and Moist characterized as the old-fashioned, polarized, either-or of the New Left taking on the Establishment. Moist elaborates on the cultural meanings and the politics of "dropping out" as a rejection of the futility and violence of the old order. To be sure, the New Left had its share of ambitious posturing and sectarian struggle, although Moist's portrayal of these traits is too sweeping. In any case, Moist's observation about the dropout culture as an alternative prompts the question of whether the Berkeley peace posters themselves share the doctrinaire rigidity Moist seems to attribute to the New Left. The psychedelic posters were available to the artists and viewers of the Berkeley peace posters as examples of the power of poster art. It may even be that, besides enriching the storehouse of poster styles, the dropout culture's suspicion of sectarian leftism tempered and provided a more complex context for the peace demonstrations of May 1970.

Matthieu Poirer argues that the Paris uprisings of May 1968 were directly linked to the international and the specifically French psychedelic avant-garde of the 1960s. Poirer draws attention to the immersive, participatory sensory disruptions of French psychedelic art that stood in contrast to the countercultural utopian dropout strain noted by Moist. May 1968, argues Poirer, drew inspiration from the ambition of psychedelic art to change "consciousness, disturbing sensorial stability." It also drew inspiration from the development of the "happening," an immersive artistic and theatrical experience that directly engaged the audience. Poirer observes that "it is no coincidence that the [French] minister of education at the time, Edgar Faure, likened May 1968 to a large 'happening.'" In French psychedelic visual art, Poirer continues, "these intransitive works appeal directly to the senses and are subsequently stripped of any cross-reference to external style other than their own phenomenological reality."[46] In the case of the Atelier Populaire, it seems evident in retrospect that the ambition of the poster artists to induce something like the direct, pure, social, and perceptual disruption of the happening and of psychedelic art was paired simultaneously with traditional poster-art appeals to militant political dissent. Such a pairing may have contributed to their peculiar power and to the unlikelihood that they would stimulate lasting social and political change. Writing of the British psychedelic scene in the 1960s, Andrew Wilson argues that "1968 marked the moment in which a belief that social and political change might happen naturally was exchanged for an understanding that such change had to be organized for, willed and made to happen. . . . However necessary thought, feeling, and imagination might be for such a revolution to succeed, the events of May 1968 exposed the split between those voyagers of inner space who believed that imagination was enough, and activists who understood that social and political struggle entailed a return to more orthodox—even Marxian—forms of analysis, conflict and action."[47]

Walter Medeiros, in contrast to Moist on the San Francisco scene and Wilson on the British 1960s, describes not so much a sharp break between the political and the psychedelic but a highly complex mix of shifting activities and people, many of whom crossed the lines of art, music, and politics. It seems likely that attendees at dance concerts and political rallies, though sometimes entirely separate populations, were often the same people. Rather than viewing the political and the cultural as two separate strains, and without simply collapsing the whole Bay Area experience of the 1960s into an amorphous mix, Medeiros sees common strains of impatience with politics and culture stimulating a variety of sometimes divergent, sometimes interactive political and cultural events.[48] Underground newspapers in the Bay Area liberally mixed sex, drugs, rock and roll, radical cultural movements, massage parlors, Black Panthers, and antiwar activism. A cover drawing in the *Berkeley Barb* for June 12–18, 1970, is typical: a pistol-packing seminude woman; a naked cop with Black Panther tattoo carrying a "Now" placard with raised black and white fists; a Capitol dome toppling in an explosion of smoke and psychedelic stars; a street fighter raising his fist; and the slogan "Only a United People's Liberation Front Can Win—The Pigs Are Everywhere."

It seems clear that there were at least some direct connections among the Berkeley peace posters of May 1970 and the poster art of the Atelier Populaire, the politics of Paris in May 1968, and the worldwide uprisings in 1968. But it seems unlikely that May 1968 was a dominating force in the rhetorical consciousness of the United States in the late 1960s or in May 1970. The war in Vietnam and turmoil over civil rights and racial justice, together with assassinations, riots, and political instability, consumed the country's attention. The assassination of John Kennedy in 1963 created grief and uncertainty. Historian James T. Patterson identifies 1965, "the year of military escalation, of Watts, of the splintering of the civil rights movement, and of mounting cultural and political change and polarization, . . . as the time when America's social cohesion began to unravel and when the turbulent phenomenon that would be called 'the Sixties' broke into view" and "lasted into the early 1970s."[49]

Every year seemed to bring new disturbances, with even the great progressive changes in civil rights—voting rights, public accommodations—bringing their own backlashes. In 1967, riots spread through the inner city of Detroit. That fall saw large demonstrations in Washington against the war. In addition to the assassinations of Martin Luther King Jr. and Robert Kennedy, 1968 brought the Tet Offensive and Lyndon Johnson's announcement that he would not run for reelection.[50] George Wallace of Alabama emerged as a candidate of the Southern backlash against civil rights, and Richard Nixon won the presidency with a promise to execute his secret plan to end the war and to restore order in the streets, along with the code words of the new Republican Southern strategy. The year 1969 brought further frustration in Vietnam and further division at home. The political and civil turmoil of the 1960s was matched by a widespread cultural upheaval. The Berkeley posters themselves have direct antecedents in Paris of May 1968, but the larger political and rhetorical climate of Berkeley in May 1970 was distinctively American.

The antecedents of the Berkeley peace posters reach beyond the recent Paris posters and the local psychedelic posters to the nineteenth-century development of the poster for commerce, art, propaganda, and protest, and further back through a long history of prints, handbills, broadsides, signs, and graffiti.[51] In the United States, poster art was employed as government rhetoric in World Wars I and II, as well as in the New Deal. The New Deal stimulated a rich government investment in public arts of all sorts, partly to develop a sense of national cohesion and optimism, and partly as a means of providing direct support to artists in all spheres— painters, writers, actors, musicians, photographers, filmmakers, designers, architects, and poster and print artists. Roger G. Kennedy and David Larkin note that in announcing the New Deal, Franklin Delano Roosevelt "was not announcing a program of princely patronage or largesse. He was, instead, inviting each of his countrymen, artists among them, to come forward in a covenant of service. Artists were among the many who needed work in 1932, and the nation needed the work artists could do."[52] Kennedy and Larkin emphasize that New Deal art was not simply propaganda or make-work, but a diverse and needed contribution to the public good "that summoned forth pride out of common experience."[53] In his pioneering 1987 study of the posters produced by artists recruited by the Works Progress Administration, Christopher DeNoon recalls the ephemerality of the posters. From 1935 to 1943, WPA artists "printed two million posters from thirty-five thousand designs." Of all those posters, only about two thousand are known to have survived. With the coming of World War II and after a red-baiting witch hunt against WPA art programs led by Martin Dies—a headline-hunting, conservative, anti–New

Deal congressman from Texas and chair of the House Un-American Activities Committee—the WPA project came to an end, and most of the posters disappeared into landfills and pulp mills, along with much other New Deal public art.[54] The Library of Congress's Prints and Photographs Division collected 907 of the WPA posters in the 1940s; that collection is now supplemented by the WPA Living Archive project, which collected additional posters from various sources. By 2012 the Living Archive had brought the total of rescued posters to 1,601.[55]

The WPA posters were created for the most part by the silk screen process. Anthony Velonis, a WPA poster artist who taught classes in the technique to students and fellow WPA artists, wrote a classic forty-four-page handbook on the method. Velonis remarked that silk screen printing, although two thousand years old, had not been used in the United States until the early twentieth century, and yet, despite the availability of various mass production printing techniques, the "Chinese stencil process has had a greater proportional growth the last five years [before 1939] than any other modern printing technique." Velonis observes that "although silk screen cannot approach the chiaroscuro of offset and lithography, it makes up for this by the richness of its pigment layer and the highly valued effect of its 'personal touch.'" And, he adds, "its initial cost is much less."[56] The WPA posters promoted public health and safety, tourism and travel, exhibitions and performances, and a wide variety of community themes (see figs. 7 and 8).

President Roosevelt spoke repeatedly about the pragmatic need to put aside class and regional conflict. FDR sounded a similar note when he encouraged tourism and travel as an economic stimulus and as a way to encourage citizens to cultivate their shared identity as Americans. The WPA poster "Work Pays America!," by Vera Bock, echoes a theme common in Roosevelt's speeches—that in the Great Depression, recovery depended on stimulating both the farmer and the laborer; each needed to be put back to work to aid the recovery of the other. While campaigning for a second term in 1936, FDR's campaign train made a short stop in Hayfield, Minnesota, where he began his rear-platform remarks by referring to tourism and regional and economic mutuality:

> I am glad to come to this section of Minnesota. I have never been on this railroad before. I hope in the next three or four years to come through by automobile and get a better idea of this country.
>
> One of the things we ought to think a lot about in this campaign is what has happened to our national point of view in the last four years. In every section of the United States we have gained the understanding that prosper-

FIGURE 7 "See America. Welcome to Montana."
Jerome Rothstein, Works Progress Administration.
United States Travel Bureau. WPA Poster Collection,
Library of Congress Prints and Photographs
Division, Washington, DC.

FIGURE 8   "Work Pays America! Prosperity." Vera
Bock, Works Progress Administration, 1936–41.
WPA Poster Collection, Library of Congress Prints
and Photographs Division, Washington, DC.

ity in one section of the country is absolutely tied in with prosperity in all the
other sections. Even back in the Eastern States and cities, they are beginning
to realize that the purchasing power of the farmers of the Northwest will have
a big effect on the prosperity of the industry and of the industrial workers of

the East. In just the same way, I know you realize that if the factories in the big industrial cities are running full speed, people will have more money to buy the foodstuffs you raise.[57]

By the late 1930s, the Federal Arts Project began to shrink, owing to changing policies and an economy stimulated by defense preparations. DeNoon writes, "In 1942, after the United States entered World War II and the nation's energies turned in a new direction, the Federal Art Project was transferred to Defense Department sponsorship and renamed the Graphics Section of the War Service Division. Under this new sponsorship, the government-employed poster artists produced training aids, airport plans, rifle sight charts, silhouettes of German and Japanese aircraft, 'Buy Bonds' booths, and patriotic posters such as one designed to encourage home-front knitting: 'Remember Pearl Harbor—Purl Harder.'"[58] The themes and motifs in the World War II posters (see figs. 9–13) are all echoed, sometimes with new meanings and valences, in the Berkeley antiwar posters of May 1970—speech and silence, the safety of children, unity across class and racial boundaries, the flag.

FIGURE 9   "Silence Means Security." Office for Emergency Management. Office of War Information. Collection of the author.

SILENCE
MEANS SECURITY

FIGURE 10   "Who Wants to Know? Silence Means
Security." US Adjutant General's Office, 1943. World
War II Poster Collection, Digitized Collections,
Northwestern University Library.

FIGURE 11   "Don't Let That Shadow Touch
Them. Buy War Bonds." Lawrence Beall Smith,
US Department of the Treasury, 1942. World War II
Poster Collection, Digitized Collections,
Northwestern University Library.

The WPA artists and their successors who created the World War II posters reinvented a genre that had first flourished in the United States, Europe, and other participating nations in World War I. Pearl James writes of the World War I posters that "mass-produced, full-color, large-format war posters . . . were both signs and instruments of two modern innovations in warfare—the military deployment of modern technology and the development of the home front. . . . Posters nationalized, mobilized, and modernized civilian populations."[59] A strikingly similar claim is offered by William L. Bird Jr. and Harry R. Rubenstein in the opening pages of *Design for Victory*, their account of home-front posters in World War II America:

FIGURE 12   "Men Working Together!" Office for
Emergency Management, Division of Information,
1941. World War II Poster Collection, Digitized
Collections, Northwestern University Library.

"World War II posters helped mobilize a nation. Inexpensive, accessible, and ever-
present, the poster was an ideal agent for making war aims the personal mission of
every citizen."[60]

The widespread view that World War II was a total war, in which victory
depended on the mobilization of national industries, had the effect of at least
implicitly justifying large-scale bombing campaigns against industrial and civilian
targets. If every citizen was a soldier, every citizen was a potentially legitimate tar-
get. The home-front posters themselves sometimes emphasized the risks of defeat,
but were largely directed at the mobilization of effort and related themes of the
"loose-lips-sink-ships" variety, war bond campaigns, and thrift. Private manufac-
turers joined the government in the production of home-front posters. "The volume of privately printed posters for factories and plant communities was said to be
greater than the number of posters issued from any and all sources during World
War I," Bird and Rubenstein write.[61] When large advertising firms brought their
talents to the poster effort, debates took shape in the Office of War Information,

FIGURE 13   "Give It Your Best!" Office of War
Information, 1942. World War II Poster Collection,
Digitized Collections, Northwestern University
Library.

which was to "review and approve the design and distribution of government posters. Eventually, contending groups within the OWI clashed over poster design.
While some embraced the poster as a demonstration of the practical utility of art,
others valued it as evidence of the power of advertising. . . . [Those] who saw posters
as 'war graphics' favored stylized images and symbolism, while recruits drawn
from the world of advertising predictably wanted posters to be more like ads."[62]
The advertising industry won the argument, partly by winning the support of
conservative members of Congress. This in turn influenced the development of
home-front posters and secured a financial windfall for advertising firms. During
World War II, the effect of posters was almost certainly exceeded by radio, motion
pictures, and print. After the war, the introduction of television contributed to the
decline of the poster as a primary mode of public and commercial communication. "Not since World War II have government, business, and labor used a wide
array of posters as a major form of communication," Bird and Rubenstein conclude.[63] Although their importance as a medium of mass communication dimin-
ished after World War II, posters did appear regularly through the 1960s, both as

FIGURE 14   "Sit-In and Demonstration (Atlanta,
Georgia): Congress of Racial Equality, 1963." The
sign carried by the man being assaulted by police
officers reads, "July 4th 1776 to 1863: Slavery.
1863–1963: Poverty. Freedom Now. L. I. CORE."
Robert Joyce Papers, 1952–1973, Historical
Collections and Labor Archives, Special Collections
Library, University Libraries, The Pennsylvania State
University. Box 6, Folder 9.

wall posters and as portable signs in citizen demonstrations for peace and civil
rights (see figs. 14–17).

The psychedelic posters, especially in the Bay Area, helped stimulate a poster
culture in the 1960s, which was amplified by the establishment of commercial
poster production for private use. College dormitory walls were commonly decorated with locally purchased, mass-produced posters that were in national circula-

FIGURE 15   "March for Peace (Washington, D.C.):
Stop the Bombing; End the War, 1965." Robert
Joyce Papers, 1952–1973, Historical Collections and
Labor Archives, Special Collections Library,
University Libraries, The Pennsylvania State
University. Box 6, Folder 12.

tion. Also in the 1960s, some fine artists, turning away from the dominant abstract
and pop styles, were creating visual art with strong social content.[64] No later than
1965, antiwar posters and paintings were in wide circulation. For the catalogue of an
exhibition of protest posters at the New School in New York, in October–December
1971, David Kunzle wrote, "The Poster of Protest was triggered by the sudden,
unexpected and massive escalation of the war in Vietnam 1965–66. By 1968
enough antiwar posters had appeared to form an exhibition (mounted in Italy) containing about seventy items. Two years later this number had more than doubled,
but there are signs that the wave of the 'commercial' poster of protest, with which
we are concerned here, is beginning to break, or to move in a new direction: the
non-commercial, utilitarian 'action' poster, modeled on the famous French student
affiches de mai."[65]

At Berkeley in May 1970, posters were simply laid out in stacks on tables in the
lobby of the College of Environmental Design. Every day, it seemed, there was a
fresh supply.[66] Lincoln Cushing says that at Berkeley the "short-lived workshop . . .

FIGURE 16   "Reaffirm America's Revolutionary Heritage;
Florida Confronts the Pentagon; Vets for Peace in
Vietnam: March on Washington Against the War in
Vietnam, October 21–22, 1967." Thomas W. Benson
Political Protest Collection, Historical Collections and
Labor Archives, Eberly Family Special Collections
Library, University Libraries, The Pennsylvania State
University. Photograph by the author.

FIGURE 17   "Save Lives, Not Face." March on
Washington against the war in Vietnam, October
21–22, 1967. Photograph by the author.

created an estimated fifty thousand copies of hundreds of works."[67] The posters were made with the approval and assistance of the University Art Museum and the faculty of the College of Environmental Design. According to Cushing, "UC Berkeley art history professor Herschel B. Chipp was a faculty advocate for the workshop artists, and he threw his support behind a student-curated exhibition at the then-new University Art Museum. It included work from the University of California, the California College of Arts and Crafts, the San Francisco Art Institute, Stanford, and other schools, as well as posters from Mexico and Paris from May 1968."[68]

In his *Art of Engagement: Visual Politics in California and Beyond*, Peter Selz, former director of the University Art Museum, recalls,

> Many antiwar posters were produced in the University Art Museum on the Berkeley campus during this time. In response to the American invasion of Cambodia in 1970, there was an outcry against the war among students, faculty, and staff at Berkeley, as at many universities in America. As director of the University Art Museum at the time, I was approached by students who wanted to turn the gallery into "campus central" for the printing of posters and the mimeographing (since this was before the time of the photocopier) of position papers. I felt that this action was called for, even though the gallery was just then the venue for two major sculpture exhibitions. . . . I placed the sculptures behind a screen to make room for silkscreen presses and mimeograph machines, feeling that, just as art is often political, politics is sometimes art.[69]

At the time, of course, these posters were not presented in any particular groupings, though perhaps the recurrence of themes would have helped some of them become recognizable while framing the others. The posters are primarily antiwar, at least by context if not by direct reference; a few refer to civil rights or the larger political process. In any case, the political themes raised in the posters do not divide neatly into mutually exclusive categories; instead, they overlap and intertwine along a variety of dimensions. Our groupings here should thus be regarded with some reservations, to avoid political or rhetorical reductionism. In any case, though the "arguments" of the posters are crucial to their meanings, the posters are not, taken one at a time or together, reducible to any single proposition.

Most of the posters are original art on silk screen; some are based on photographs, and some are produced by photo offset. Some of the art is purely typographic. The color palette is typically limited, giving the posters a simplicity, directness, immediacy, vividness, and in some cases a beauty that is striking. All of it provides symbolic dimensions through pure design by creating tone and stance.

One cluster shows a variety of Vietnamese or more broadly Asian themes, with strong appeals for identification. In "This Is Life—This Cuts It Short" (see fig. 18), a mother and child (life) are juxtaposed against a rifle (this cuts it short) gripped in an unknown hand. The mother and child are clearly Asian but are also familiar, in a pose that might suggest a Madonna and child. The child directs its gaze at the viewer, with a look that, in context, must suggest alarm, even fear. The theme of violence directed against women and children recalls the My Lai massacre of the previous year, and of continuing stories of civilian deaths in Vietnam, which was the subject of the widely circulated "And Babies? And Babies" poster created in December 1969 by members of the Art Workers Coalition. "And Babies" reproduces a photograph of the My Lai massacre showing a row of bodies, including several babies; printed on the poster is the question "And babies?" and the answer, "And babies," from an interview of Paul Meadlo, one of the US soldiers involved at My Lai, conducted by Mike Wallace of CBS News. The "And Babies" poster had been commissioned by the Museum of Modern Art and the Artist Workers Coalition; when a proof copy of the poster was shown to William Paley and Nelson Rockefeller, trustees of MoMA, the poster was rejected and the MoMA director was fired. The Artist Workers Coalition printed the posters on its own, and they were quickly circulated in New York and around the world. Copies of the poster apparently arrived in Berkeley in late December 1969 or early January 1970.[70]

"Does He Destroy Your Way of Life?" (fig. 19) repeats the appeal to identification, but adds a theme of distance. A peasant farmer, shown in silhouette, follows a buffalo pulling a plow. The viewer may identify with this homely, harmless figure as a fellow creature, but, with the buffalo and the conical straw hat, the poster also denotes something exotic and remote, amplifying the question "Does he destroy your way of life?"—a question clearly addressed to an American viewer who has been told by his government that the Vietnam War is required to halt worldwide Communist aggression. On the contrary, the poster seems to assert, this is a figure whose simplicity should prompt us to identify with his humanity, but whose remoteness should convince us that he is not a threat to us, on the other side of the world.

The danger to the Vietnamese implied by figures 18 and 19 is more directly asserted in plate 4, "Vietnamization," which shows a photograph of a bloodied mother and infant, apparently collateral damage from a US attack. These depictions of victims of war's violence are a counterpart to a common theme of war posters, in

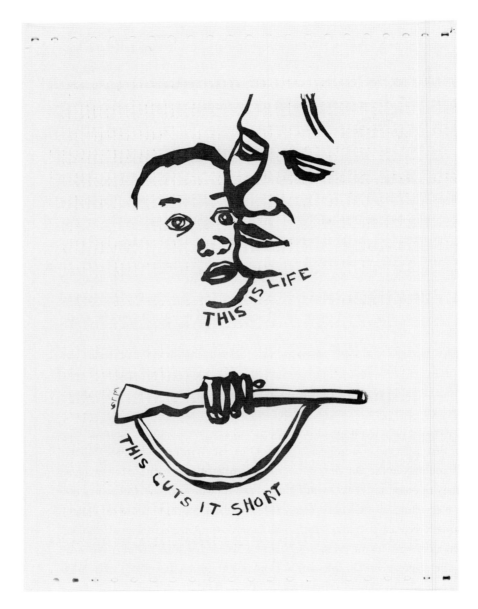

FIGURE 18   "This Is Life—This Cuts It Short."
Thomas W. Benson Political Protest Collection,
Historical Collections and Labor Archives, Eberly
Family Special Collections Library, University
Libraries, The Pennsylvania State University.

FIGURE 19 "Does He Destroy Your Way of Life?" Thomas W. Benson Political Protest Collection, Historical Collections and Labor Archives, Eberly Family Special Collections Library, University Libraries, The Pennsylvania State University.

which images of victims or potential victims are offered as justification for war (compare plate 4 to fig. 11, "Don't Let That Shadow Touch Them"). The "Vietnamization" poster also uses the trope of irony by juxtaposing a verbal quotation with the actuality that it implies—a trope also at work in "And Babies." Such comparisons appear frequently in the posters, sometimes by using contrasts within the imagery, sometimes in contrasts between the image and the words. Juxtaposition is a key rhetorical structure in generating meaning. Ironic juxtaposition motivates plate 5, "It Became Necessary to Destroy the Town to Save It"—the title draws on a quotation from an on-camera interview between a US Army major and AP reporter Peter Arnett. The poster features a photograph by Paul Avery of a terrified, elderly Vietnamese couple.[71]

Other posters showing Vietnamese or Southeast Asian settings are "Nature Is Beautiful (So Is Human Nature) Conserve It" (plate 2), one of several posters gesturing toward the developing environmental movement, and in this case suggesting a link between the environmental movement and the peace movement from which it seemed in danger of diverging; and "Free Asia—U.S. Get Out Now" (plate 6); "Asia for Asians!!" (plate 7); "Her Suffering for Our Comfort? STRIKE" (plate 8);

"Vietnam: Spilled Blood Split the Country" (plate 30), again an image of a Vietnamese mother, this time with a dead or injured baby—the country split is the United States; and "Unity in Our Love of Man" (plate 33). "Did You Vote for This? Who Did?" (plate 13) is based on a 1968 AP photograph of the bodies of US Marines on Hill 689 in Khe Sanh, South Vietnam.[72] The image of a woman carrying a child in plate 30 is apparently based on a news photograph of a Vietnamese woman carrying a horribly burned baby "after an accidental napalm raid twenty-six miles southwest of Saigon."[73]

"Did You Vote for This? Who Did?" is an indirect invocation of the political order in the United States, and, for those who remember, a reminder that both Lyndon Johnson (in 1964) and Richard Nixon (in 1968) won the presidency with promises of peace—which were then contradicted by their actions—and that the evident futility of the war drove Lyndon Johnson from the presidency in 1968. The "Who Did?" is a rhetorical question, implying that because both winning candidates—and in 1968 both Hubert Humphrey and Richard Nixon—promised peace, in effect no one voted for "this." Similarly, "Vietnam: Spilled Blood Split the Country" refers to the double collateral damage of the war—to innocent civilians in Vietnam and to the civic peace of the United States. Implicitly, such appeals are not a rejection of the political order in the United States but a lament for its weakening by the war. Plate 26, "War Is Unhealthy for America," similarly implies that the war is damaging the people and America itself, including its civic life.[74]

"Asia for Asians!!" (plate 7) shows an Asian man raising the middle finger of his right hand to the viewer. The image is startling, funny, and defiant, and it draws its thematic power from the same spirit that informed "Yankee, Go Home" at the time of America's Cuban incursions earlier in the 1960s, and from the developing debate about black power and African American leadership of the civil rights movement in the United States. The lettering of the poster is vaguely Asian, and may, as in the psychedelic San Francisco posters, take an extra moment to decipher. Yet it is in English, and the gesture of the subject is familiar. He wants and deserves his autonomy, but he speaks our language. The comic, mocking, but unthreatening tone of the poster contrasts with the solemnity of many of the other posters, but it shares with them a strong implicit appeal to the moral value of human autonomy, which by implication America's occupation of Southeast Asia denies.

"Unity in Our Love of Man" (plate 33) pictures a young Asian boy carrying a younger boy on his back—both are apparently refugees of the war in Vietnam—and is an appeal for identification across cultural difference. To whom does "our" refer in this poster? Presumably to the older boy in the image, who is helping another child, and to the viewer, whose love for children unites the viewer with the

boys. But "our" is not defined explicitly, and it could refer as well to a love of humanity as a basis to reunite the opposing factions in the United States. The ambiguity
gives this simple poster a resonance that lingers and deepens beyond a first impression for a viewer who is in a position to contemplate and reflect. In the cluster of
posters depicting Asian peoples, but clearly addressed to American viewers, both
identification and difference are invoked to argue for peace as the transcendent
responsibility. The unity suggested is one of human identity, and seems to imply
no sense of partisan support for the North Vietnamese or Vietcong—a position
taken by some in the antiwar movement.

   A few of the posters directly refer to the shootings at Kent State, or refer more
broadly to the victimization of young people by the regime, the culture, and the war
(see fig. 20).[75] Figure 20 shows Ohio National Guard soldiers firing at the distant
students, who are not visible in the photograph.

   Some of the posters directly challenge or mock politicians (see fig. 21). At least
two of the posters object to war profiteering. Figure 22 (also plate 22) singles out
General Electric, which was a producer of weapons. Another poster, "Money
Talks—Boycott War Profiteers" (plate 21), shows a dollar bill with a gagged George
Washington; the bill is decorated with a peace sign.

FIGURE 20   "Kent State University, May 4, 1970."
Thomas W. Benson Political Protest Collection,
Historical Collections and Labor Archives, Eberly
Family Special Collections Library, University
Libraries, The Pennsylvania State University.

FIGURE 21 "No Nixon Agnew War." Thomas W.
Benson Political Protest Collection, Historical
Collections and Labor Archives, Eberly Family
Special Collections Library, University Libraries,
The Pennsylvania State University.

Among the human costs of war suggested by the posters was the damage the conflict had done to American democracy. Typically these posters employ visions of patriotism in the cause of peace, directly addressing the notion that the peace movement was subversive and was encouraging the intransigence of Ho Chi Minh and the North Vietnamese, thus directly endangering American troops. Dissent in time of war always risks the perception of disloyalty.[76] In the posters at Berkeley in 1970, patriotism is not, with a few exceptions, mocked or disparaged; rather, the posters repeatedly assert that "Peace Is Patriotic" (see fig. 23; also plate 35). The legitimacy of opposition to the Vietnam War is a key theme, and suggests the extent to which the Nixon administration (and the Johnson administration before it) and its supporters challenged the patriotism of opponents to the war.

The posters often spoke to the coalition of the peace and civil rights movements—a coalition that was showing signs of strain at the time. Figure 24, "Kent State. Augusta, Georgia," refers to the National Guard shootings at Kent State University on May 4, 1970, and to a riot that took place in Augusta, Georgia, on May

FIGURE 23 "Peace Is Patriotic." Thomas W. Benson Political Protest Collection, Historical Collections and Labor Archives, Eberly Family Special Collections Library, University Libraries, The Pennsylvania State University.

11–12, 1970. The uprising in Augusta erupted in response to the murder of a young African American boy at a local jail and the apparent collusion or indifference of authorities.[77] Six African American men were shot to death by police and the National Guard in the night of rioting. All were shot in the back.

Again and again the posters evoke the power of human speech, both rhetorical and poetic, and call the viewer to take action (see fig. 25). In none of the posters calling for action do we find the figure of revolutionary violence that Nixon, Rhodes, Agnew, and Reagan were warning against in their own depictions of college students. Instead, speaking and writing are figured as modes of existential and civic action—the virtuous action of a moderate middle fed up with the war—or as the nonviolent direct action (boycott, don't pay your telephone taxes) of a more radical but still peaceful dissent. Sometimes the action called for is individual and personal; sometimes, it is collective, and yet the collectivity is never pictured as a mere crowd.[78] Such images and appeals recall Norman Rockwell's image *Freedom of*

FIGURE 24 "Kent State. Augusta, Georgia."
Thomas W. Benson Political Protest Collection,
Historical Collections and Labor Archives, Eberly
Family Special Collections Library, University
Libraries, The Pennsylvania State University.

FIGURE 25   "Speak Out, You Got to Speak Out
Against the Madness, You Got to Speak Your
Mind." Thomas W. Benson Political Protest
Collection, Historical Collections and Labor
Archives, Eberly Family Special Collections Library,
University Libraries, The Pennsylvania State
University.

FIGURE 26 / *opposite*   "Save Freedom of Speech.
Buy War Bonds." Norman Rockwell. Office of War
Information Poster no. 44. Washington, D.C.: United
States GPO. World War II Poster Collection, Digitized
Collections, Northwestern University Library.

Speech (see fig. 26), after FDR's Four Freedoms speech of 1941.[79] In the context of
the moment, the Berkeley posters themselves were a mode of action.[80]

In none of the Berkeley posters do we find a call to stone throwing, arson, or
rioting—all of which did happen on the fringes of the antiwar movement.[81] Where
collective speech is evoked, it is not that of a conspiracy or a mob but the action of
peaceful citizens exercising democratic responsibility. Hence, it may be reasonable
to suggest that although the posters by their nature and practice convey simple and
straightforward messages, and thus may seem to exist essentially as propaganda,
many of the Berkeley posters invoke a reflexivity about their own persuasion and
call for discussion beyond the poster—asking not merely for belief or action, but
for speech, participation, deliberation. In a distinction between *propaganda* and

persuasion, Garth Jowett and Victoria O'Donnell define propaganda as "the deliberate, systematic attempt to shape perceptions, manipulate cognitions, and direct behavior to achieve a response that furthers the desired intent of the propagandist." In contrast, they suggest that in persuasion, the attempt to change attitudes or behaviors is "interactive," "transactional," and consensual.[82] Similarly, rhetorical theory often posits its ideal standard as a situation in which, if the persuasion is not back and forth or face to face, it is at least adaptive to the genuine needs of the listener. It also accepts an obligation to bilaterality (willingness of the speaker to listen and change), mutual consent, mutual risk, freedom of expression, and some level of reasonableness.[83]

Perhaps the most forceful of such images is the poster of Richard Nixon as a character from the cartoon strip *Peanuts*, sucking his thumb and holding his security blanket to his cheek (see fig. 27). The caption is an allusion both to the *Peanuts* character Linus van Pelt, invoking the wisdom that "security is a thumb and a blanket," and to Richard Nixon's speech of November 3, 1969, in which he described what he called his quest for peace in Vietnam and said, "And so tonight—to you, the great silent majority of my fellow Americans—I ask for your support."[84] That speech was itself the subject of controversy at the time, just months before the events of May 1970, and was widely seen as another pledge by Nixon to ignore antiwar protesters. The speech came a little more than three weeks before the revelations of the My Lai massacre.[85]

President Nixon's silent majority speech of November 1969 came just a year after his election, and less than a month after a national antiwar "Moratorium," a massive peace protest of October 15, 1969, with rallies drawing a million people around the country. It was followed by another, on November 15, 1969, with especially large demonstrations in San Francisco and on the Mall in Washington, DC. Nixon's speech was announced on October 13, just two days before the first Moratorium. By the time of the speech, opposition to the war was widespread in mainstream American politics and had attracted the backing of national political leaders, both Democratic and Republican. And yet the speech was widely seen as an attempt to deflect support from the Moratorium by suggesting that peace advocates were merely a radical fringe.

The "Silent Majority" poster is an implicit refutation of Nixon's "radical fringe" maneuver. By invoking a shared knowledge—a knowledge shared by artist and viewer—of the iconic and mostly nonpolitical *Peanuts* comic strip, the poster identifies its roots in a nonthreatening, traditional America, while at the same time mocking Nixon as an infantile tyrant. The theme of "security" had been the touchstone of the New Deal. Later many liberals, and then 1960s cultural and political

FIGURE 27 "Security Is a Silent Majority." Berkeley, California, 1970. Thomas W. Benson Political Protest Collection, Historical Collections and Labor Archives, Eberly Family Special Collections Library, University Libraries, The Pennsylvania State University.

radicals, resisted what they took to be the complacent cultural longing for the sub-urban security of the Eisenhower years.[86]

The analytical implications of the "Silent Majority" poster run through many of the other posters. Similarly, across the humanities and social sciences, the perception that the Nixon administration was threatening democracy itself prompted theoretical and empirical work aimed at understanding—and in some cases resisting—the threat.

The silent majority speech—the subject of the "Silent Majority" poster—was coincident with a disciplinary paradigm shift in American rhetorical studies, some of it prompted directly by the silent majority speech, as in the case of a critical examination by Professor Robert P. Newman of the University of Pittsburgh. Newman's article, "Under the Veneer: Nixon's Vietnam Speech of November 3, 1969," appeared in the *Quarterly Journal of Speech*, the field's flagship journal, in June 1970. In Newman's analysis, Nixon's speech was deliberately confrontational, and needlessly so, because it confronted the peace advocates in an attempt to gain the support of the centrist "silent majority" and the potentially "emerging Republican majority" made up of traditional Republicans and the angrier fringe who had voted for George Wallace. Newman examines in detail Nixon's deliberative rhetoric, which he describes as "casual and obfuscating logic that defies belief. . . . Here it is, all over again, the false dilemma, the black or white position, the collapse of all alternative strategies into the one most offensive and easiest to ridicule. Only two choices: my plan, or the cut-and-run cowardice of the rioters in the streets."[87] Newman concludes that "neither his rhetorical strategies nor his substantive arguments were sound."[88] In those days, it was unusual for rhetorical scholars to engage directly with the rhetorical strategies and the substantive arguments of an ongoing debate, and to do so, as Newman did, by holding a president to standards of logic, substance, and ethics. Others had written of Richard Nixon, often with disapproval, and of such political figures as Senator Joseph McCarthy, but Newman was catching something more: he was joining a deeper, multidisciplinary shift in academic discussion of the war, of the president, and, by implication, of the business of rhetorical criticism itself. In general, academic rhetorical critics had observed the proprieties of being disinterested judges of rhetorical tactics and strategy; typically, they granted the speaker the substance and confined their critical analysis to the skill with which the speaker pursued his or her agenda, a stance encouraged by the scientism of the early twentieth-century roots of the discipline, by traditions of academic civility, and by reaction to the dangers of the postwar red scare. But internal developments in the discipline, and changes in the larger society, especially the civil rights movement and the Vietnam War, changed that. Younger academics were beginning to explore how they might bring their own disciplinary perspectives to the resolution of current controversies, opening political culture to broader debate and holding leaders to account.[89] The discipline was responding in its own way to precisely the issues raised in the "Security Is a Silent Majority" poster. Rhetorical scholars were struggling to make explicit the theory that is implicit in the poster.[90] The poster calls Nixon to account by implicitly appealing to rhetorical commonplaces of civic responsibility. The rhetorical scholars of the period worked to articulate in disciplinary terms what, exactly, was at stake in the issue the poster encapsulated, and what that meant for the discipline and its own civic responsibilities.

Robert Newman's analysis of Nixon's November 1969 Vietnam address was soon followed by others. In a 1971 essay in the *Quarterly Journal of Speech*, Hermann Stelzner posits that Nixon's speech was structured as a quest narrative—which, as an implicit structure familiar to listeners, might well carry some force. He grants that the speech allows Nixon to buy time, but argues that the implicit appeal to the myth of the quest reveals Nixon as a failure, inflated with braggadocio and self-admiration. And yet he concedes, "This speech was not offered to the public as a literary work. It deals with practical political problems and if evaluated accordingly it accomplishes some objectives. Although divisiveness in the political community remains, Nixon gains an audience and time. He finds listeners who will respond to his words and images. He gains a firmer possession of the policy he lays out before them and makes himself ready for the next series of events he must deal with in Vietnam."[91]

The next year, Karlyn Kohrs Campbell published an essay asking whether the president's speech met the standards he set for himself: "In the President's opinion the people of the nation should be told the truth. The three criteria the President explicitly suggests are truth, credibility, and unity, and he later implies a fourth criterion based on responsibility and ethical principles." In a detailed analysis of the address, Campbell finds that Nixon violates each of these principles—he lies and deliberately sows disunity and division, violating fundamental principles of ethical rhetoric. "Although this speech fails to meet the President's criteria of truth, credibility, unity, and responsibility, the most significant criticism is that this rhetorical act perpetuates the myths about America, which must be debunked and shattered if we are to find solutions to the problems that threaten imminently to destroy us."[92]

Together, the essays by Newman, Stelzner, and Campbell suggest a skeptical distancing from the authority of the presidency, and their work begins to invoke standards of judgment that go beyond the pragmatic assessment of rhetorical effectiveness.

In late 1972, Forbes I. Hill's "Conventional Wisdom—Traditional Form—The President's Message of November 3, 1969" was published in the *Quarterly Journal of Speech*. Hill's essay is a reply to Newman, Stelzner, and Campbell, and it is framed as a detailed analysis of Nixon's speech from the point of view of "neo-Aristotelian" rhetorical criticism.[93] Hill writes, "Neo-Aristotelian criticism compares the means of persuasion used by a speaker with a comprehensive inventory given in Aristotle's *Rhetoric*. Its end is to discover whether the speaker makes the best choices from the inventory to get a favorable decision from a specified group of auditors in a specific situation. It does not, of course, aim to discover whether or not the speaker actually gets his favorable decision; decisions in practice are often upset by chance factors."[94] Hill offers here a clear statement of neo-Aristotelian practice, and in his essay he provides a spirited account of how successfully President Nixon applied "the available means of persuasion" to fracture the electorate and buy time for his presidency, without actually offering any progress on the promised ending of the war. But the discipline, while not abandoning its interest in Aristotle's foundational *Rhetoric*, was already moving rapidly in other directions, seeking to understand rhetoric from the point of view of the citizen whose judgment was being solicited, recovering marginal voices, asking questions about the ethics of persuasion, investigating the rhetorical action of non-oratorical forms, pressing forward on the close reading of rhetorical texts, and inquiring about empirical matters such as the preparation, circulation, and reception of rhetoric. The instrumental view of rhetoric advocated by Hill was challenged by a constitutive view that investigated what rhetoric was asking us to be, and to be together.

These developments that were reshaping the field of rhetorical studies had as their focus the question of whether the duty of the scholar of rhetoric is chiefly to advise the rhetor how to achieve a higher level of success, whatever his or her ends, or whether the scholar is in some larger sense responsible to the civic order in which the speaker acts, taking into account those whom the speaker addresses (or ignores) and the standards and resources of civic discourse. Hill's narrower perspective, for the previous forty years or so dominant, now shared the field with the larger view, with effects the discipline is still developing.

The paradigm shift—or perhaps it would be better thought of as the broadening of the paradigm, or the multiplying of paradigms—questioned the dominant assumption that the rhetorical scholar's perspective should be limited by the speaker's purposes; that rhetoric worth studying was typically that of important or influential figures; that rhetoric was confined to discourse—to speech and writing; that rhetorical scholarship studied a case in order to add to the more general store of knowledge that is rhetorical theory. The new critics, branching off in a variety of directions, insisted on opening criticism to the point of view or the interests of the audience, or the civil society, or even to others not directly addressed but implicated in a rhetorical action. They questioned the aims, the assumptions, and the veracity of the rhetor. They studied marginalized rhetors. The new critics explored rhetorical action in strikes, marches, demonstrations, graphic arts, architecture, film, and music. They argued over whether rhetorical knowledge was sometimes better understood in close attention to the particular without having to justify itself by an appeal to theory. The renewal brought a new attention to close textual analysis and, at the same time, a more original historical attention to issues of the production, authorship, circulation, and reception of texts. The roots of these changes can be found, all of them, in rhetorical scholarship before the 1960s, but it was then that the rapid diversification began to be widely visible. These changes, while not altogether displacing "traditional" or "neo-Aristotelian" criticism, gave fresh energy to rhetorical studies.

This attention to the process of civic discourse itself—including but not restricted to the merits of a given argument—runs through the posters circulated in Berkeley in May 1970, just as the discipline (of course invisible to the world of action—those who were making and viewing the posters in Berkeley in May 1970) was learning how to adapt to the revolutions of the 1960s. The "Security Is a Silent Majority" poster points directly to this set of issues. The poster's ironic complaint is that Nixon is failing in his discursive obligation to be straight with the American public, that the president is retreating instead to the security of a silent majority—presumably grateful that it is silent, in contrast to those who spoke out against the war—and that he is assuming that silence meant support for his views. Other interpretations of the silent majority theme are of course possible, but they are not suggested by the poster, and so do not become directly a part of its rhetoric.

The notion of a silent majority, both the phrase itself and the ideas it suggests, especially when invoked by a president, had a history that is curiously intertwined with President Nixon's speech. The idea that it is the president's job to speak for those who do not or cannot speak for themselves was elaborated by Woodrow Wilson, who saw the presidency as in part a rhetorical office. Jeffrey Tulis has given the term "rhetorical presidency" to a development that he attributes to Theodore Roosevelt and Wilson—the practice, which in Tulis's view is a constitutional innovation, of speaking over the heads of Congress to the people, with the effect of assuming legislative leadership. Woodrow Wilson claimed that it was his role to not simply shape to public opinion but also to give forceful articulation to the public's undeveloped hopes and needs. This goes beyond simply treating public opinion polls as plebiscites. According to Tulis, Wilson understood himself to be "an interpreter of the popular will. . . . 'Interpretation' involves two skills. First, the leader must understand the true majority sentiment underneath the contradictory positions of factions and the discordant views of the mass. Second, the leader must explain the people's true desires to them in a way that is easily comprehended and convincing."[95] According to Tulis, most presidents since Wilson have adopted, with good or ill effects, some version of the rhetorical presidency. It seems clear that Richard Nixon, in his invocation of the "silent majority," was enacting, at least in part, the role of interpreter of the unvoiced or discordant views of the masses.[96] But there is more to it than that—or perhaps it is a misinterpretation by the poster artist. In the speech, Nixon also seems to approve of the silence of the silent majority, and it is to this suggestion that the "Security Is a Silent Majority" poster appears to object—the suggestion that the public should be quiescent while the president pursues a war in Americans' name.[97] Some of the most famous World War II posters had also counseled silence, but in that context, silence was meant to protect secrets that the enemy might overhear (see figs. 9 and 10).[98]

The phrase "silent majority" is given two primary definitions in the authoritative *Oxford English Dictionary*. In the first sense, the phrase refers to the dead, in which sense it was used in 1874 as a heading in *Harper's Magazine*. In its second sense, the silent majority is "the mass of people whose views remain unexpressed, esp. in political contexts; those who are usu. overlooked because of their moderation," and it is in something like this sense that Nixon employs the phrase, which was used, in the earliest example cited by Oxford, by historian C. V. Wedgwood in *The King's Peace: 1637–1641*, published in the United States in 1956. Wedgwood writes, "The King in his natural optimism still believed that a silent majority in Scotland were in his favour and 'only wanted a hand and arms' to rise against the Covenanters."[99] Wedgwood does not attribute the phrase "silent majority" to the king, but does attribute the analytical point of view, in very much the sense in which President Nixon invokes it, to this seventeenth-century English monarch. In *Safire's New Political Dictionary*, William Safire, who had been a Nixon White House speechwriter, notes John F. Kennedy's use of the phrase in his 1956 *Profiles in Courage*, which Nixon almost certainly read, and adds that the phrase had been used earlier in 1969 by Vice President Spiro Agnew and by presidential historian Theodore White.[100] Agnew, according to Safire, said on May 9, 1969, "It is time for America's silent majority to stand up for its rights, and let us remember the American majority includes every minority. America's silent majority is bewildered by irrational protest."[101]

When Kennedy invoked the phrase in his *Profiles in Courage*, he celebrated courageous American politicians, of whom he writes, "These men were not all on one side. They were not all right or all conservatives or all liberals. Some of them may have been representing the actual sentiments of the silent majority of their constituents in opposition to the screams of a vocal minority; but most of them were not."[102] In the context of the debate over Vietnam, it is also worth noting that Kennedy celebrated politicians who did not simply invoke the silent majority as presumptive support for their views, but opposed it—although Kennedy, like Nixon and Agnew, contrasted the silent majority with "the screams of a vocal minority," as if there were no articulate and reasonable oppositional minority.

The Berkeley posters clearly insist that they are part of a responsible and patriotic movement against the war, a group that Richard Nixon, Spiro Agnew, and Ronald Reagan brush away by depicting all Vietnam War opponents as a vocal minority of "irrational protest." And yet with growing force from the mid-1960s on, a large segment of responsible American leadership and public opinion had arrived at a conscientiously informed and influential opposition to the war. Robert Kennedy, Eugene McCarthy, and other senators were by 1968 calling for an end to the war, and Nixon himself had been elected with a promise to bring the troops home.

Two of the posters depict Vice President Agnew, and both do so in the context of commenting on and encouraging political speech. Agnew was an unusually active surrogate for Nixon in 1969, giving a series of intensely partisan speeches in which he devoted special attention to attacking university opponents to the Vietnam War. In these speeches, Agnew vigorously criticized student speech and protest behavior, and he later extended his attacks to include a preemptive warning to broadcast journalism. Agnew's speeches were certainly the source drawn on by the poster artists in the two Agnew posters in the collection, and the speeches would have formed part of the context of interpretation that viewers applied to the posters. Part of Agnew's method was to employ the ancient rhetorical figure of the part for the whole—what the Greek rhetoricians called *synecdoche*. In Agnew's rhetorical world, the most objectionable war protesters stood in for all war opponents; a version of this tactic was used by Nixon in his November 1969 speech on Vietnam, and it was especially galling to the majority of opponents to the war who did not engage in extreme forms of protest, but whose opposition was depicted as radical and disloyal. Whatever the merits of these opposing views, all this was vividly present at the time and was condensed in the two Agnew posters.

Spiro Agnew's 1969 speeches are well represented in *Frankly Speaking: A Collection of Extraordinary Speeches*, which begins with a speech to the Young Presidents' Association in Honolulu, in May 1969, and traces his increasingly aggressive campaign as a presidential surrogate. Some of Agnew's speeches were actually written by Nixon's White House speechwriters—a practice that continued after Gerald Ford replaced Agnew, who was forced to resign in disgrace for corruption in office.[103] On November 13, 1969, with specific reference to Nixon's silent majority speech, Agnew used an address to the Midwest Regional Republican Committee in Des Moines to warn television broadcasters away from commentary on the president's speeches:

Monday night, a week ago, President Nixon delivered the most important address of his Administration, one of the most important of our decade. His subject was Vietnam. His hope was to rally the American people to see the conflict through to a lasting and just peace in the Pacific. For thirty-two minutes, he reasoned with a nation that has suffered almost a third of a million casualties in the longest war in its history.

When the President completed his address—an address that he spent weeks in preparing—his words and policies were subjected to instant analysis and querulous criticism. The audience of seventy million Americans—gathered to hear the President of the United States—was inherited by a small band of network commentators and self-appointed analysts, the *majority* of whom expressed, in one way or another, their hostility to what he had to say.[104]

Agnew's Des Moines speech was widely regarded not simply as a criticism of the television networks but also as a warning to them that the Nixon administration had the power to damage their interests. According to Rick Perlstein, "it worked. 'Everyone is scared about licenses,' a network executive explained to the *Los Angeles Times*. 'You can't have a television station without a government license, and you can't have a network without stations.' Two days later, the peaceniks gathered in Washington, D.C., for the New Mobilization's 'march against death.' Conspicuously absent were live network cameras."[105]

Plate 15 depicts the face of Spiro Agnew, with a smile of apparent self-satisfaction, perhaps wearing a Mao jacket. The poster declares, "Big Brother is watching you, so do something." The "Big Brother" allusion is to George Orwell's novel *1984*, and it refers to the widely reported complaints about a national security state in which the government, in a state of endless war, patrolled the speech and actions of citizens. Agnew had taken on the time-honored role of hatchet man during an election campaign—a role Agnew extended into his vice presidency. The Big Brother poster complains about the intimidation and encourages the viewer to defy it by "doing something" (the phrase itself an allusion to a joke in circulation at the time, "don't just do something, stand there").[106] The spirit of "so do something" in the face of government oppression mirrors the comic antics of Jerry Rubin and Abbie Hoffman, who, when called to testify by the House Un-American Activities Committee, mocked the proceedings by rejecting the usual tactics of protest, such as taking the First or Fifth Amendment, or making moral or constitutional objections to the committee. Rubin and Hoffman showed up in costume—Rubin as an

American Revolutionary War soldier and Hoffman as Santa Claus—and answered questions with mock-serious nonsense. The notion of refusing to hide from government surveillance, sometimes by resorting to comic defiance, runs here and there through 1960s dissident rhetoric, and it had shown up again in 1968 when Rubin, Hoffman, and their Yippie party suggested that they might lace Lake Michigan with LSD before the Chicago presidential nominating convention of the Democratic Party.

"An Effete Corps of Impudent Snobs" (plate 17) is also an allusion to Vice President Agnew, who used the phrase in his anti-dissident speeches and became well known at the time for his snide, faux-clever phrasing and aggressive alliteration, as in "nattering nabobs of negativism" and "pusillanimous pussyfooters." The iconicity of "An Effete Corps of Impudent Snobs" is perhaps overloaded. Agnew first used the phrase "effete corps of impudent snobs" in reference to the October 1969 Moratorium in a speech at New Orleans on October 19, 1969: "Education is being redefined at the demand of the uneducated to suit the ideas of the uneducated. The student now goes to college to proclaim rather than to learn. The lessons of the past are ignored and obliterated in a contemporary antagonism known as the generation gap. A spirit of national masochism prevails, encouraged by an effete corps of impudent snobs who characterize themselves as intellectuals."[107]

Shortly afterward, and after his remarks prompted a mixed reception, Agnew elaborated the charge in a speech to a Pennsylvania Republican dinner at Harrisburg on October 30, 1969. Agnew said,

> Now, we have among us a glib, activist element who would tell us our values are lies, and I call them impudent. Because anyone who impugns a legacy of liberty and dignity that reaches back to Moses is impudent.
>
> I call them snobs, for most of them disdain to mingle with the masses who work for a living. They mock the common man's pride in his work, his family, and his country. It has also been said that I called them intellectuals. I did not. I said that they characterized themselves as intellectuals. No true intellectual, no truly knowledgeable person, would so despise democratic institutions.
>
> America cannot afford to write off a whole generation for the decadent thinking of a few. America cannot afford to divide over their demagoguery, to be deceived by their duplicity, or to let their license destroy liberty. We can, however, afford to separate them from our society—with no more regret than we should feel over discarding rotten apples from a barrel.[108]

In the poster, the standing figure wears a swallowtail coat and waistcoat and a shirt with a stand-up collar, and strikes a mock-elocutionist pose, one arm folded across the breast, the other flung out toward the speech balloon in which ". . . an effete corps of impudent snobs . . ." appears in blue paint over a background of red and white stripes, one of the many flag allusions in the collection. The pose is a stereotypical version of a nineteenth-century stance that might in that century have been taught in a class on elocution.[109] The head of the figure is a donkey—possibly a reference to the Democratic Party, and perhaps suggesting the imputation that Agnew is referring to Democratic senators who opposed the war, although in fact a number of Republicans and former Republican (later independent) Wayne Morse did so as well. If this reading of the poster is more or less an accurate sense of its contemporary meaning, then it, too, is criticizing the Nixon administration for attacking a core function of democratic deliberation—congressional speech— while asserting the importance of opposition by citizens and politicians.

There is a simpler reading. It may be that the poster is meant to depict Agnew as a political jackass, who in referring to the Moratorium movement calls the anti- war students "an effete corps of impudent snobs" and casts his own words as red- white-and-blue patriotism. This reading would discard the iconography of the Democratic donkey, but it is a more direct reading, and it is supported by the con- text in which Spiro Agnew was understood at the time. The question of the poster's "meaning" illustrates some of the difficulty of appealing to the iconographical his- tory of design elements in a rhetorical interpretation. From an iconographic per- spective, the donkey image is suggestive. From a rhetorical perspective, we are probably forced to admit interpretive defeat: the poster is not simply ambiguous but overburdened with iconographic potential. Is the head a Democratic donkey or an Agnew jackass for a 1970 viewer? The poster is interesting as a window into the moment, but in the moment it was probably more ambiguous than a political poster should be.

Several of the posters designed in or circulated in Berkeley in May 1970 empha- sized, among other themes, the obligation of citizen participation, protest, and speech. Plate 11, "All His Parents' Love and Devotion Did Not Save the Life of This Boy," reproduces in posterized black and red the photograph of Jeffrey Miller lying dead at Kent State. Under the photograph, the poster lists suggested actions— writing and petitioning government representatives, boycotting economic goods, refusing to buy bonds or pay war taxes, writing letters, calling talk shows, talking to neighbors.[110] Plate 49 depicts a soldier or police officer standing over a figure he has just subdued, or perhaps shot, and asks the viewer, "Remember Peace? Speak

Out to End War."[111] Plate 49 might at first seem to refer to a photograph by Eddie Adams, who won a Pulitzer Prize for his 1968 photograph of Vietnamese general Nguyen Ngoc Loan shooting a Vietcong prisoner, his hands manacled behind him, on a Saigon street. The prize-winning photograph was taken at the moment of execution; another photograph in the series shows General Loan standing over the dead man a moment later, as he turns away from the body, and it is this later, less familiar photograph that might seem to have inspired plate 49. Instead, the poster is based on a photograph that appeared on the front page of the *Berkeley Barb* of May 8–14, 1970, next to the headline: "RISE UP ANGRY!!! NO MORE LYING DOWN." The photograph shows a police officer in riot helmet, standing over a figure curled on the ground at his feet; the officer holds a revolver upward in his right hand; from his left hand a long wooden nightstick angles down from crotch level. He stares in the direction of the camera.[112] When the *Barb* photograph was appropriated for the poster, a message of angry uprising was replaced by a call for peace and citizen advocacy.

Plate 57 asks the viewer to "write for peace," showing a hand holding a quill pen, evoking the Committees of Correspondence of the American Revolutionary era. Plate 58 declares, "Speak out, you got to speak out against the madness, you got to speak your mind." Plate 59 shows a steer marked as cuts of beef, with the legend "He didn't protest either." Plate 60, showing human figures as cogs in a machine, warns, "Don't be a silent part of the war machine—speak out against Cambodia," directly resisting silence and the assumptions of silence as assent in Richard Nixon's use of the "silent majority." The human figure as part of the machine is reminiscent of Charlie Chaplin in *Modern Times* (1936) and of Fritz Lang's *Metropolis* (1927), with their warnings of the inhumanity of modernity. "Write for Peace" directly prompts citizen action. At the same time, as labor and political organizers understand, persuading a person to take even a very small action on behalf of a cause is likely to intensify identification with the cause—even if the action itself has little other measurable effect.

Plate 61 reproduces the familiar "child at gunpoint" photograph from the Warsaw ghetto, with Nazi soldiers herding Jews into captivity; featured in the center of the photograph is a young boy with his hands raised in surrender.[113] The poster announces, "America is a democracy only as long as it represents the will of the people. Unite for peace!! Things *you* can do," followed by a list of suggested actions; the same list, in a poster also by the Kamakazi Design Group, appears in plate 11. Plate 62 is printed in photo offset by Berkeley Graphic Arts, as are plate 11 and, probably, plate 61. Plate 62 proclaims in large type, "You are already involved":

The myth of the "silent majority" is dead. We are all involved. It is no longer possible to avoid our responsibilities and to seek refuge in silence and apathy. Name calling, blind patriotism, and simplistic political clichés cannot negate 40,000 American war dead and the destruction of Southeast Asia and its people; nor can they negate the toll which this war and its consequences have inflicted upon American society. No escape can be found in the abdication of political responsibility. Each of us must examine the situation and recognize his position.

In the past few weeks, students and faculty from the nation's universities have taken positive measures to end U.S. military involvement in S.E. Asia. In an unprecedented effort to educate ourselves and the general public to the issues of the war and the implications within our society, the campus community has demonstrated the need for active participation. Writing, speaking, and lobbying have prevailed across the country. Such legitimate and necessary dissent must be reinforced by public support.

Personal action in a country as complex as ours often seems futile. But personal commitment is crucial for our society to face its problems and overcome them. Our form of government is based upon our legislators' representing our convictions. We must make these convictions known to them. Let us move together to bring to the attention of our fellow men their obligation to act and to support those who have made a commitment to ending the war. We must each recognize our personal responsibility to act, and move accordingly. We are already involved.

The statement is signed by students and faculty at California universities and colleges, in a gesture that suggests involvement, identification, legitimacy, and potency.[114] The four actions suggested are coupled with clip-off coupons with addresses and a space for the signer's name and address. Viewers are invited to write to their legislators; support the Vasconcellos bill in the state legislature; support the McGovern-Hatfield amendment in Congress; or contribute money to the organizing committee.

The appropriation of photographs in so many of the posters suggests to their viewers a rootedness in actuality and their access to—but independence from— the larger culture of commercial images. Every photograph bears a documentary testament. The photographs appropriated in the Berkeley posters—some in large photo-offset posters, some rendered in silk screen images—bring the larger world close in something stronger than an analogical way, as they are rooted in actuality, which is itself part of the rhetorical problem addressed by peace rhetoric: the war seems so far away, the suffering so abstract. These photographs support the larger appeals of the posters to involvement, the connection of here and there, then and now, pressing spectacle to the work of action and agency.[115]

Plate 63, "America Says: Actions Speak Louder than Words," adds layers of complexity to the theme of speech and silence. The poster shows a high-contrast halftone print of Richard Nixon glowering at the viewer from under his brows, his jowls heavily shadowed with the dark rasp of his unshaved jaw, his widow's peak aimed at the camera. This is the famously menacing Nixon of the Herblock cartoons, the Nixon of whom it was said (wrongly) that his mere face lost him the presidential debate with John Kennedy in 1960. Nixon's left hand points aggressively out of the frame. The poster is a direct reference to the widely familiar British recruiting poster from World War I, sometimes titled in one of its variations "Your Country Needs You" (1914), with a steely Lord Kitchener glaring—and pointing—out at the spectator over his huge mustache (see fig. 28).

The Kitchener poster was famously imitated in the James Montgomery Flagg poster "I Want You for the U.S. Army" (1917), with Uncle Sam pointing out of the picture to the potential recruit. Kitchener and Uncle Sam are recruiting; Nixon seems to be saying "Shut up!" or "I'm watching you!" and echoing the Big Brother theme of plate 15. In context, the poster turns Nixon's appeal for the support of the silent majority into a demand for silence. Carlo Ginzburg explores the Kitchener poster in part by tracing the context, effects, and historical roots and descendants of the poster. He notes especially Kitchener's eyes and pointing finger, tracing to Pliny the Elder descriptions of a painting of Minerva "who viewed the viewer no matter where he looked from," and an image of "Alexander as Zeus, with projecting fingers and holding a thunderbolt," an effect achieved by "extreme foreshortening."[116] The reference to the Kitchener poster in the Nixon poster generates an ironic frame, comparing the forthright patriotism of the remembered Kitchener with the devious, warlike Nixon, who speaks words of peace. The audience of the Nixon poster is reminded that the president's actions contradict his occasional claims that he is merely seeking "peace with honor."

As in most of the posters, the words speak directly to the viewer. The "speaker" in most of the posters is implicitly a collective voice of dissent and not merely that of the artist, who is anonymous. In only a few cases is the author of the verbal text in one of these posters explicitly identified, as in plate 62, "You Are Already Involved."

FIGURE 28 "Britons [Lord Kitchener] Wants You.
Join Your Country's Army! God Save the King."
Alfred Leete. Imperial War Museum, London.
Art.IWM PST 2734. Used by permission.

Plate 63, printed by the Pacific Rotaprinting Company, extends the list of suggested citizen actions that had appeared in other posters. From additional text in
the poster, it appears that the "actions" that "speak louder than words" are both
Nixon's and the viewer's:

> For the last nine years and three presidents America has been hearing that
> troops were being brought home from Southeast Asia as quickly as possible,
> yet today there are still more American Soldiers in Southeast Asia than ever
> before. How can we continue to believe in Nixon's desire to end the war when
> his every action denies this? Troops come and go; there are games of escala-
> tion and de-escalation, and the war keeps growing.
>
> Likewise, most Americans say they are against the war, yet continue to do
> "business as usual." The actions of American students speak louder than
> Nixon's words. Universities everywhere are closing down and working against
> the war, and will do so until the last soldier is home. If Americans are really
> eager to end the war let us take direct action.

The call for "direct action" and the contrast between "action" and "words" in the
poster are, from the point of view of communication theory, complex and perhaps
at risk of incoherence. In fact, the list of suggested "actions" includes a variety of
acts of speaking and writing. Each of these is part of our political and conceptual
vocabulary—speech as merely symbolic in contrast to material action, speech as a
mode of action, action as a mode of speech, speech as an incitement to action, communication as an ethical alternative to violent action.[117] In the context of the poster,
the general call to take action, to do something, probably makes the appeal rhetorically coherent under the circumstances.

The Kitchener poster is echoed in plate 65, "Join Now," in which a figure wearing a top hat decorated with a peace symbol points at the viewer. The figure is
apparently an allusion to the Uncle Sam of the James Montgomery Flagg "I Want
You" poster, who wears a top hat bearing a star and points toward the viewer. The
figure in "Join Now" appears to have an olive twig in its mouth. The peace symbol
was first designed by Gerald Holtom for the Campaign for Nuclear Disarmament
in Great Britain, where it was used as the primary graphic symbol for the 1958
Aldermaston march. The symbol was quickly adopted by the antinuclear movement in the United States and absorbed into the wider peace movement that grew
up in response to the growing war in Southeast Asia. The symbol itself was created
by combining the semaphore signs for N and D—Nuclear Disarmament. In the

"N," the signaler holds the two flags downward and outward from the body. In the "D," the signaler holds the right hand straight above the head and the left hand straight down.[118]

In plate 18, "Run *This* One Up Your Flagpole, Dick!," the peace symbol appears on a flag partway up a flagpole seen in diminishing perspective. The poster at first look seems defiant and obscene. The poster might appear at first to be simply a sophomoric dirty joke, but even to get the joke elicits more shared knowledge than that. The dirty joke part is the allusion to "your flagpole," along with "Dick," a slang term for penis and a familiar insult when used in direct address as an epithet.

"Dick," of course, refers to Richard Nixon, who was sometimes known to be referred to by his friends as Dick Nixon, but to his opponents Dick Nixon was always "Tricky Dick." Nixon was first elected to Congress with a red-baiting campaign against Congressman Jerry Voorhis of California. In 1950, Nixon ran a similarly red-baiting campaign against Helen Gahagan Douglas, referring to her as "the Pink Lady" and printing election fliers on pink paper, in an election for the United States Senate. Douglas referred to Nixon as "Tricky Dick" to draw attention to his campaign tactics, and the appellation stuck—for his opponents. Nixon won the Senate campaign and two years later was selected by Dwight D. Eisenhower to be his vice presidential running mate.

The "run this one up your flagpole" is a rude way of saying "give peace a chance," and it is an allusion to Madison Avenue jargon widely scorned among intellectuals in the 1950s and 1960s—the slang alluded to in the poster was "Let's run it up the flagpole and see if anyone salutes."[119] The Madison Avenue reference serves as a reminder of the merchandising of Nixon in the 1968 campaign, chronicled by Joe McGinniss in his *The Selling of the President*.[120]

The flagpole poster, especially when seen in context, is itself part of the discussion of the politics of discourse—of the substitution of Madison Avenue manipulation for democratic deliberation—that runs through many of the posters and is a core theme of McGinniss's book. The flagpole poster is not simply mocking the president but is a rude claim for peace and a challenge to the degradation of democratic deliberation.

Plate 64 addresses the viewer with the admonition "Don't be 1 of the silent majority—speak out." Rows of silent, grim faces, eyes closed, form the background and contrast to one pleasant, moonlike face whose eyes are calling to an unseen audience, its mouth open in speech. Plate 66 shows the faces of five figures, apparently women and men, who are evidently talking outward toward the viewer or out of the edge of the frame; the words "speak out against the war" are carved out around the figures. The faces and words seem to share the same shape, substance, color, and sentiment. Each of the speakers addresses a slightly different direction, perhaps suggesting the unity in diversity that was a theme in many of the posters.

Questions of unity and diversity, of individuality and collective action, run through many of the posters—explicitly in many, implicitly in others. The issue is clearly present in the posters that call on American audiences to identify with Vietnamese victims of the war, but it is also at stake in asking American viewers to put aside their own differences for the sake of collective action in a worthy cause. The problems of unity and diversity are an ethical and practical problem for those dissenting from the war in 1970; these organizers are attempting to manage the competing and sometimes divergent interests of race, gender, culture, and issue—of green, black, red, white, pink—and turn them into a coalition to end the war.

American gender relations were undergoing rapid change in 1970, and certainly in the Bay Area, but the changes do not seem to be taken up as a theme in the posters, in which women suffer, mourn, mother, comfort, and inspire (as in plates 3, 4, 8, 11, 28, and 30).[121]

The theme of speaking out, being involved, or remaining part of the silent majority presented the viewer with similar structures of decision. Every person who joined a protest march, signed a petition, or cast a vote was called on to reflect on the ethics of joining a large collective movement that by its very nature could not always match the exact views and preferences of every individual participant. How much identity of interest was enough to provoke collaborative action? Because this issue was so salient to the politics of the 1960s, and because the movement was always in danger of fragmenting, it is not surprising to see appeals to unity and reminders that there was no such thing as inaction. Inaction, the posters insisted, was not an option. The silent would be counted as part of the silent majority: "You are already involved."

The theme of American race relations is explicit in several of the posters. Some called for unity between the peace and civil rights movements. In plate 52, "Unite Against the War," a yin-yang circle contains the image of a raised fist, the symbol of "black power," and a raised hand making a "V" gesture—at the time a peace symbol.[122] The call for unity between the two movements illustrates something of the split that had developed between white liberals and black civil rights advocates in the 1960s. James Patterson observes, "The trend toward black direction of civil rights activities, even if it excluded whites, had been relentless since the travail of the Mississippi Freedom Democratic Party at the Democratic National Convention in 1964."[123] In 1966, on a freedom march from Memphis, Tennessee, to Jackson,

Mississippi, days after march organizer James Meredith was shot by a white man in Hernando, Mississippi, the newly elected leader of the Student Nonviolent Coordinating Committee, Stokely Carmichael, made famous the phrase "BLACK POWER!" Patterson notes that "the quest for black power was a more or less inevitable result of the dynamics of civil rights protest in the 1960s. . . . Proponents of black power insisted simply that white people could not be trusted to help them. It followed that black people had to control their own political and economic institutions. If whites felt abandoned, that was too bad. If they grew violent, blacks must be ready to defend themselves."[124]

Many African American leaders had advocated for peace in Vietnam: "Since the middle of 1966, [Martin Luther] King had publicly opposed the Vietnam War, which he called 'a blasphemy against all that America stands for,' . . . but his opposition seemed to be having no effect on public opinion besides dampening support for civil rights and earning him the enmity of President Johnson."[125] Many other African American leaders opposed the war, and many leading white opponents of the Vietnam War were strong civil rights advocates, and yet a working coalition of the peace and civil rights groups did not develop. When the posters were being produced and circulated at Berkeley in May 1970, powerful outside forces and internally fragmenting pressures within both the peace and civil rights communities were making the formation of a strong multi-issue movement unlikely, according to Simon Hall. During this period, writes Hall, "a genuine peace and freedom coalition was not established and . . . even cooperation between the two movements was relatively rare."[126]

James Baldwin, in his 1961 book *Nobody Knows My Name*, observes, "Men do not like to be protected, it emasculates them. This is what black men know, it is the reality they have lived with; it is what white men do not want to know. It is not a pretty thing to be a father and be ultimately dependent on the power and kindness of some other man for the well-being of your house."[127] In a speech to ten thousand people in the Greek Theatre on the Berkeley campus on October 29, 1966, Carmichael echoed Baldwin's admonition: "Now, then, in order to understand white supremacy, we must dismiss the fallacious notion that white people can give anybody their freedom. No man can give anybody his freedom. A man is born free."[128] In the same speech, Carmichael condemned the war in Vietnam, partly on the grounds that it drafted black men as mercenaries, who were then killing and being killed in the name of an "illegal and immoral" white man's war.[129]

In October 1966, the same month that Carmichael spoke on the Berkeley campus, Bobby Seale and Huey Newton formed the Black Panther Party for Self-

Defense in Oakland, California, on the border with Berkeley. The Black Panther Party had a brief and spectacular life. In 1968 Bobby Seale became one of the "Chicago Eight," who were prosecuted for their role in the agitation surrounding the Democratic National Convention that summer. The Chicago Eight became the Chicago Seven when Seale was separated from the case. Seale mocked and interrupted Judge Julius Hoffman, who ordered him gagged and shackled in the courtroom and later sentenced him to prison for contempt.[130] The Chicago trial, which lasted from September 1969 to February 1970, was national news and was highly visible in Berkeley.

Plate 53, "Seize the Time," shows the face of Bobby Seale, whose book on the Black Panthers, *Seize the Time: The Black Panther Party and Huey P. Newton*, was published in 1970. Seale's image is from a photograph. His face appears thoughtful, brow slightly furrowed with worry or concentration, one shoulder slightly cocked. The image is in high-contrast black and white. Plate 54, "Free All Political Prisoners," showing a raised fist above a manacled wrist attached to a chain, is a clear reference to Seale, the Black Panthers, and the Chicago Seven.

Another sort of unity is appealed to in posters that gesture toward the counterculture community with peace symbols in psychedelic designs, as in plate 36, "Peace Now"; plate 41, "Come Together for Peace"; and plate 65, "Join Now."

Just as at the thematic level the posters legitimize opposition or appeal for unity, they gain much of their energy at the formal level through features of opposition, contradiction, and contrast, on the one hand, or implied coherence, unity, and reconciliation on the other. Rhetorical figures of contrast appear in the foundational claim that "peace is patriotic" (plate 35), a sentiment that would seem obvious but in the national imagination is anything but obvious. Similarly, "Her Suffering for Our Comfort? STRIKE" (plate 8): our conventional public memory of "suffering," "comfort," and "strike" would most obviously take the form of "Our suffering for their comfort? Strike," in the context of a labor struggle. The remixing of the formulation into something using familiar elements in an unexpected—but immediately comprehensible—way introduces an implicit pattern of comparative judgment that is breaking free of habitual ways of thinking.

The rhetorical structures of contrast and re-visioning called upon so frequently in the posters are strongly represented through the American flag as a motif. The infantile Nixon of "Security Is a Silent Majority" clutches an American flag to his cheek, suggesting appeals to patriotism as a pathetic retreat from engagement. "Peace Is Patriotic" (plate 35) implies that the war's supporters have used patriotism, and the flag, to improperly silence their opponents.[131] Plate 44, depicting an

American flag in which the red stripes are rifles and the white stars are warplanes, shows the flag upside down, a symbol of distress and an accusation of hypocrisy.[132] Plate 58, "Speak Out, You Got to Speak Out Against the Madness, You Got to Speak Your Mind," shows a flag distorted in a way reminiscent of the psychedelic posters, with an expressionistic sense of agony and urgency.

Plate 19, "Recycle Nixon," shows an American flag design in green and suggests a unity of purpose between the antiwar movement and the growing environmental movement. Earth Day had been celebrated for the first time on or about April 22, 1970, and it inspired millions of Americans and led to teach-ins at universities across the country. It was still too soon—perhaps it is still too soon—to understand the extent to which the rapidly growing environmental movement was an enlargement of the liberal-progressive coalition for civil rights, civil liberties, and peace, and the extent to which environmentalism represented a diversion or diffusion from radical politics. In any case, environmentalism was a potent presence in April and May 1970, and allusions to green flags would have been widely understood.[133]

The posters frequently suggest government hypocrisy, contrasting administration claims or shared public ideals with actual behaviors. "Did We Really Come in Peace for All Mankind?" (plate 47) shows the rounded horizon of the moon's surface in the foreground; over the horizon hangs the Earth in dark space. The question asked refers to the first human landing on the moon by Neil Armstrong and Buzz Aldrin on July 20, 1969. The Apollo 11 astronauts left a plaque bearing the words "We came in peace for all mankind" and displaying Nixon's signature.

The flag and other patriotic motifs may be said to be at once conservative and radical in their rhetoric. They draw on collective public memory, with which they assert their own affiliation, while making their own claim on our memory of antiwar rhetoric in the sixties. The images of the flag and other patriotic motifs perhaps also draw on and appeal to a collective memory of American radical rhetoric that goes back to the early Republic. They are, in other words, recalling America to its ideals and suggesting that the failure to live up to those ideals amounts to hypocrisy. David Walker's abolitionist *An Appeal to the Coloured Citizens of the World* (1829) charged that American slavery was at odds with the Declaration of Independence.[134] Walker wrote,

> See your Declaration Americans!!! Do you understand your own language? Hear your language, proclaimed to the world, July 4th, 1776—"We hold these truths to be self evident—that ALL MEN ARE CREATED EQUAL!! that they

are endowed by their Creator with certain unalienable rights; that among these
are life, liberty, and the pursuit of happiness!!" Compare your own language
above, extracted from your Declaration of Independence, with your cruelties
and murders inflicted by your cruel and unmerciful fathers and yourselves
on our fathers and on us—men who have never given your fathers or you the
least provocation!!!!!![135]

The appeal to the ideals of the Declaration was employed later by Abraham Lincoln
in the Gettysburg Address; by Frederick Douglass in "What to the Slave Is the
Fourth of July?" (1852); in the Declaration of Sentiments (1833) of the American
Anti-Slavery Society; and in the Declaration of Sentiments (1848) of the Seneca
Falls Convention for women's rights.[136] Such appeals to American memory, which
are frequent in the posters, are not radical objections to American ideals but calls
for the nation to live up to those ideals. These posters are dissident, but their dissent affiliates itself with tradition and the nobility of the American aspiration to
freedom, justice, equality, and peace.

The posters are ephemeral, and their very existence speaks to the urgency of the
present moment. Yet they assert their own identity with a longer and a larger public
memory. They speak to present history with both contemporary and historical
images, in a way that is part of their rhetoric—their argument—as well as their art.
The ephemerality of the posters, combined with their immediacy (fresh every day)
and localism (made here on campus), carries a strong rhetorical flavor of vernacular authenticity. The posters often have an artistic and technical distinction beyond
the capacity of non-artists, achieving a style that is professional yet vernacular. This
impression is reinforced by the on-strike-keep-it-open ethos of the campus in those
days, in which scholars and students from many disciplines were bringing their
own talents and perspectives to the movement. At the same time, despite the
ephemerality of the physical poster, its creator was making gestures to larger
frameworks in remembered time and imagined futures. Through their sheer artistic distinction and their aesthetic excesses, the posters give pleasure and make a
genuine moral argument.

The rootedness of the posters is, in part, an exercise in the instant recognition—
sometimes followed by a double take—that a successful poster inspires. The icons
and motifs are familiar, and they are rich with shared memory. Similarly, the posters based on photographs have a rootedness both in familiar journalistic images
and in the link to physical actuality—a witnessing to the suffering that is known,
real, inescapable. The posters thus avoid the conventional suspicion that they are

merely utopian dreams of perfection or universal pacificism. They object to policies, practices, and persons in the here and now, and they offer what appears to be
already-known evidence supported by shared commonplaces.

I have identified as crucial to the posters the claim that they are part of a legitimate deliberation about American policy, and that they are calling on their viewers
to be part of that deliberation. Under the circumstances of 1970, the antiwar movement and the universities as part of civil society share this task as well. To be sure,
the posters contain other important themes, and in some cases take what might
seem an angrier, more disaffected tone. But overwhelmingly, the posters call for
peace, and they call for speech.

Similarly, the posters do not merely ask for diversity; they also collectively represent and constitute diversity. They claim legitimacy, membership, potency, and
voice as part of civil society. Even the angriest few of the posters seem to express
indignation at the denial by the Nixon administration of the legitimacy of dissent.
That is a remarkable achievement in a country as weary, angry, and divided as
America in 1970.

Just as the posters are a call to speech and action, they are themselves a mode of
speech and action, and this is not incidental to their rhetorical force. Each of the
posters, for example, asks not only to be seen but also to be shown. The posters
were produced in quantity and given away free. Soon they were appearing in windows on campus and throughout the city; they were shown on walls and fences,
and they found their way to homes, dormitory rooms, and offices. When shown in
these ways, the posters spoke doubly—they spoke for themselves, and they spoke
for the person who exhibited them (see fig. 29). Figure 29 shows some of the
Berkeley posters affixed to the fence of a private home on Grant Street in Berkeley
in May 1970.

We are now distant from the time and place of the circulation and reception of
the Berkeley posters; we are likely to see them as history rather than as rhetoric,
and their remoteness may lend these posters a sort of nostalgia or prompt us to
wonder why then but not now, years into another unpopular war. But we may also
lose touch with the rhetoric of these posters because we are seeing them together,
in reproductions, and clustered thematically and iconographically. In some ways,
this does justice to their rhetoric—they are full of puns, jokes, and layers—but the
posters nevertheless speak with a direct simplicity and boldness that does not
require extensive contemplation to grasp their point. Still, seeing them all at once,
we can lose something of the material directness of the posters.

FIGURE 29   "Antiwar and Protest Posters: Posters
Mounted by Citizens on House Fences." Berkeley,
California, 1970. Thomas W. Benson Political
Protest Collection, Historical Collections and Labor
Archives, Eberly Family Special Collections Library,
University Libraries, The Pennsylvania State
University. Photograph by the author.

The posters speak as images, as messages, and as objects. They are cheap, paper, free, anonymous, ephemeral. As physical objects, they are fairly fragile, but they can travel through their publics, then stand temporarily in one spot. Often the paper in these posters was being reused. The Tom Roberts poetry poster (plate 56) is printed on poster stock; the reverse is an out-of-date psychedelic calendar. Many of the posters were printed on the reverse of used tractor-feed computer printer paper. Sometimes they were printed on two sheets of computer paper, held together by a perforation that ran across the center of the poster.

The obviously cheap, local, and immediate materiality of these posters, their ephemerality, their occasional graphic distinction, their vernacular wit, and their anonymity gave the posters an authenticity and force that are unusual. It makes a difference that they are posters: several of the posters, given their simple content and form, might have served instead as newspaper cartoons, or perhaps full-page ads; instead, they circulated as objects, and in the case of the silk-screened posters, as handmade objects. They carry a presence, an aura, an eventfulness that would not have been present in the same way had they simply been published—which might have given them a wider audience but which would have resulted in a different rhetoric.

Picking up one of these posters and posting it in a visible place in one's home or office or carrying one, mounted, in a peace march was an act of solidarity with a local movement. The anonymity of the artist was itself a form of testimony. The large number of artists itself spoke for a solidarity that nevertheless contained distinctive voices, and these in turn made possible an act of testimony in displaying the poster for others to see. This doubling of the voice of the poster is something more than bumper-sticker advocacy; displaying one of these posters was more immediate and collective than displaying FDNY on the window of a pickup or "support the troops—bring them home now—alive" on the window of a Volvo.[137] Some of the posters were printed directly on corrugated cardboard sheets. In this form they could be posted with tacks or tape, or they could be tacked to a handle and used as signs in a public demonstration; the posters printed on paper could easily be taped or glued to cardboard and used the same way.

None of these posters has the prestige, and none has the artistic aura, of Ben Shahn's 1968 McCarthy for president poster, or Shepard Fairey's "Hope" poster for Barack Obama, but they do have other qualities that lend them special rhetorical potential.

The Berkeley posters are ephemeral, but they are not simply homemade—even the modest production requirements of silk screen on old computer paper require a level of technical and artistic skill and materials of production that are beyond our own daily practice. The posters have a compelling visual power even today. Some of the simplest of the posters are the most beautiful—rendered in a single color, most often blue, red, green, magenta, or a combination, and in a style that asserts rather than denies that they are produced from hand-cut stencils.

The posters permitted testimony by both artist and exhibitor in a way that official, professionally produced campaign posters do not. Because the posters were anonymous, free, and circulated from a central location, they also implied that they

were the result of a cooperative enterprise—not that they were written by a committee, but that they were individually produced with a sense of common purpose.
Though the posters were anonymous, they were not secretly produced, because
they were circulated from a common location. This, at least, is the rhetorical suggestion of the posters themselves as they circulated from Wurster Hall in May
1970. As a historical matter the posters cannot be confidently said to represent a
measure of opinions, although they certainly suggest a range of opinions or effects,
from "we are your worst nightmare" (in just a few cases) to "we are the center, the
citizens" (in most cases). As a rhetorical matter, the posters do speak as testimony
to strong convictions and as moral calls to belief and action.

We Are Exporting Democracy

The Berkeley posters appear to exercise a complex generic performance. The
generic inventiveness and the quite specific historical, cultural, and geographic
rhetoric of the posters can, in part, be shown by comparing them with contrasting
types, such as commercially produced political graphics and street graffiti. The
Berkeley posters are "political," and yet they are different in style and appeal from
generic, professional political campaign posters. Figure 30 shows "yard signs" (a
staple of elections in the United States) with ready-made lawn spikes that also serve
as interior framing. In figure 30, some of these yard signs appear in Pennsylvania
in 2007, outside a church that was serving as a polling place.

In comparison, figures 31 and 32 show campaign posters from Rome, Italy, in
2004 and 2005, where some wall spaces are made available for licensed posters.
Campaign posters, though the artist may be anonymous and usually is, are always
speaking not only for but also on behalf of an institutionalized client, although that
effect too can be subverted. Figure 33 shows a Roman antiwar poster from the same
period—"We Are Exporting Democracy"—featuring President George W. Bush,
Silvio Berlusconi, and one of the infamous Abu Ghraib photographs. The poster is
a parody of the typical campaign poster, with a slogan and the smiling faces of the
politicians.[138]

Rome has a long history of political dissent, still exercised as it has been since
the beginning of the sixteenth century at the talking statues, most notably at the
statue called Pasquino (the source of our English word "pasquinade," denoting a
political lampoon). The statue was dug up in an excavation in Piazza Navona in
1501. Pasquino, like the other Roman talking statues, is decorated with anonymous

FIGURE 30   Campaign yard signs. Pennsylvania,
2007. Photograph by the author.

FIGURE 31   Political campaign posters for Silvio
Berlusconi. Rome, June 2004. Photograph by the author.

FIGURE 32   Political campaign posters for Partito
Comunista Rifondazione. Rome, June 2004.
Photograph by the author.

mockeries of authorities, typically in verse form, and still attracts the lively attention of Romans and tourists passing by. Figures 34 and 35 show Pasquino in May
2007, more than five centuries after he started talking to the people of Rome. The
Pasquino postings are anonymous—alluding to a tradition where, in a former age,
to post a message on the statue was to risk punishment by the papal authorities if
the author should be discovered.

Political graffiti do not carry the sort of institutional stability usually attached to
a campaign poster. Graffiti, whether drawn freehand or applied with a stencil and
spray paint, bring an entirely different mode of address from protest or campaign

FIGURE 33   "Esportiamo democrazia" (We are
exporting democracy). Rome, June 2004.
Photograph by the author.

posters. A graffito is always evidence of an event, and its anonymity always carries
a whiff of vandalism, transgression, and defiance. Heller and Vienne list graffiti, in
the form of what they call "street slogans," as among the "one hundred ideas that
changed graphic design." They note that in France in 1968, the "disruptive slogans" were "hard to ignore because they popped into view at the oddest angles,
when least expected. Handwritten, spray-painted, they were untidy, the hurried
quality of their letterforms suggesting haste, momentum, speed—characteristics
that are meant to raise a red flag in our brain and make us extra vigilant." They
observe that "in our modern age of mobility, distraction is the new attention."[139]

FIGURE 34   Pasquino. Rome, May 2007.
Photograph by the author.

FIGURE 35   Pasquino. Rome, May 2007.
Photograph by the author.

Graffiti have become a commonplace part of the urban visual scene. Joe Austin and Norman Mailer seem to agree that modern urban graffiti are all political, in at least the larger cultural sense. Joe Austin writes of "writing" graffiti that

> writing was inspired by the political mass movements of the 1960s, by the utopian strains swirling within the contradictory mixture of counter-culture and commercial popular culture, by urban youths' own sense of the narrowing possibilities for social acceptance and economic mobility in a postindustrial city, and by the traditions created within earlier youth formations, which they inherited. Part of the larger, dispersed, and ongoing struggle for public space among marginalized groups in the United States, writing quickly became a forum for social criticism. It also served as a public arena for ritualized rebellion and rage for both youths and the adults who challenged them, particularly those adults who fostered an alliance in the "war on graffiti."[140]

Mailer, in a largely elegiac essay on urban graffiti, catches something of the cultural menace with his observation that "perhaps it is the unheard echo of graffiti, the vibration of that profound discomfort it arouses, as if the unheard music of its proclamation and/or its mess, the rapt seething of its foliage, is the herald of some ongoing apocalypse less and less far away. Graffiti lingers on our subway door as a memento of what it may well have been, our first art of karma, as if indeed all the lives ever lived are sounding now like the bugles of gathering armies across the unseen ridge."[141]

By their nature graffiti are not, like posters, portable, or distributed for further posting in homes and offices, but meet the viewer on the street, or on the side of a train (see fig. 36). Graffiti are less easily destroyed than posters, although in most cases the removal of graffiti by scrubbing, blasting, and over-painting is a constant activity in affected cities. Figures 37–49 show a sample of graffiti found along Via Cavour, a main street in Rome, after a massive peace march stimulated by a visit to Rome by President George W. Bush on June 4, 2004, and extending here and there through the war in Iraq and Afghanistan. Via Cavour, which begins near the main train station, ends on the Via dei Fori Imperiali, within view of the Colosseum, in the heart of historic and tourist Rome. The Roman antiwar graffiti resemble the work of the Berkeley posters, and make the similarities and differences perhaps more telling than a comparison of the Berkeley posters with graffiti in general.

Silvio Berlusconi's Italy was for a time one of the "willing allies" of the United States in the war on terrorism. It seems clear from the Italian street protests that

FIGURE 36   Urban graffiti. Reggio Emilia, Italy,
April 15, 2012. Photograph by the author.

hostility to the United States could be efficiently communicated with images of
President Bush, whose visage in these graffiti stands for terror, torture, and imperial war. The antiwar graffiti of the Roman street could be quickly applied to a wall
in the midst of a large demonstration that obscured the action of the graffiti makers, who appear to have been working with stencils that could be mixed and
matched to produce variations. In figure 44, the "USA Terror" stencil has been
applied next to a silhouette of the famous Abu Ghraib photograph; in figure 45, the
"USA Terror" stencil appears next to a profile of Bush.[142]

The graffiti are imposed on a wall—someone else's wall. The Berkeley posters
were sometimes imposed on the walls of others, but they appear at least as often to
have been displayed on one's own wall. When graffiti are transformed from an
imposition to a display, they have begun the transformation from graffiti to mural.
These implicit modes of address become part of the experience of the posters and
graffiti as they are encountered in the street. Both posters and graffiti have the
capacity to challenge, though by themselves they cannot overthrow the omnipres-
ent visual experience of normal life in what Debord calls the spectacle—the situation of modernity.[143]

FIGURE 37   "Stop War Now." Graffiti stencil.
Rome, June 2004. Photograph by the author.

The defiance and the strongly anti-Bush tone of these graffiti, and their mode of articulation and address, help us see how rooted the Berkeley antiwar posters of May 1970 were in the rhetoric of their time and place, and how moderate was the appeal of many of them, even when they were mocking President Nixon. The Berkeley posters are, to be sure, protest posters, but they are not revolutionary; nor do they express the implied impotence and marginality of much protest. Rather, they identify their authors and their owners as participants. They dissociate from Nixon and the war, but they identify with the normal political process, with the larger society, and with the Vietnamese people.

In the context of the times, of the counterculture and the New Left, of SDS, the posters take a decidedly moderate, reformist, liberal democratic position. They resist the negative stance implied by the terms "dissent" and "protest," though

FIGURE 38   "Stop [Bush]." Graffiti stencil. Rome,
June 2004. Photograph by the author.

structurally that is the position they occupy, since they are objecting to current
policies and practices, and rhetorically the genre of "protest" framed their reception. The posters' moderation is all the more striking when we recall that much
more radical positions were available locally and nationally in May 1970, by which
time the counterculture of drugs, music, and lifestyle was well under way and the
New Left had been active for a decade. In fact, as the best histories of the New Left
and the SDS make clear, by May 1970 the SDS itself had moved in just ten years
through several turnovers of leadership and had burned through reform to resistance, then invoked revolution, and had burned out in a fratricidal war between the
Weather Underground and the Maoists of the Progressive Labor wing of the party.
By March 1970, a group of Weather Underground would-be terrorists moved into
an apartment at 18 West Eleventh Street in Greenwich Village and began making
bombs; on March 6, the bombs exploded as one of them was being wired, killing

FIGURE 39   "Vattene!" (Go away!) Rome, June
2004. Photograph by the author.

three of the bomb makers. Thus hysterical movement rhetoric was certainly available for the poster artists to draw on, but for the most part they did not do so.

What, then, are we to make of the politics of the posters? It may be that they
show the resilience and persistence of a core antiwar democratic liberalism that is
sometimes obscured by the media at the time, which was attracted to the more
sensational edges of dissent as exemplified by the SDS and its violent fringe.[144] The
posters are perhaps all the more remarkable for avoiding the extremes of the antiwar movement, which by this time had seen strains of "bring the war home" and
"Ho Chi Minh is going to win."[145]

There are exceptions. A poster, apparently from Berkeley in May 1970, preserved in the collection at Vancouver, shows a nighttime scene of figures surrounded by smoke, or perhaps clouds of tear gas, with the words "Fight ROTC.

FIGURE 40   "No Blood for Oil." Graffiti stencil.
Rome, June 2004. Photograph by the author.

Join SDS."[146] Any attempt at an interpretive assessment of the rhetoric of the
Berkeley posters must be offered with a few caveats. The posters at Penn State University form a large collection; the collection at the University of British Columbia
is somewhat larger, as is a recently mounted exhibit at the Oakland Museum of
California; and the collection in the archives at the University of California, Berkeley, is even larger and more diverse.[147] The collections do not show a unified ideo-
logical, political, or rhetorical line on the part of the artists. In any case, the viewers
of these posters—the point of the rhetoric, after all—saw much smaller samples.
A single viewer saw perhaps only one or a few out of the larger collections eventually assembled. The variety among the posters as a whole was sufficiently large that
viewers could pick and choose among political positions and tone from the most
radical to the most moderate. And, of course, we must keep in mind the ephemer-

FIGURE 41   "Stop War. Join the Resistance." Rome,
June 2004. Photograph by the author.

ality of the posters themselves; it is quite possible that some have not survived.
Still, what remains is enough to astonish us with its artistic energy and to admon-
ish us that the extremes of the antiwar movement did not represent the whole of
the American opposition to the war, even in Berkeley.

In the collection of the Oakland Museum, some 183 Berkeley workshop posters
from 1970 are now on digital display.[148] Several of the posters in the collection,
which was curated by Lincoln Cushing, are absent from the Penn State holdings.
Among those are a few with more militant appeals that challenge any claim that all
the Berkeley posters are mildly civic. One shows a rat carrying a rifle, with the text,
"Fascist Infested!"[149] An American flag with a dollar sign in place of stars flies
above a domed building in the background. In another, the Kent State photograph
of Alison Krause is overlaid with the text "AVENGE." "It's the Real Thing for S.E.
Asia" shows part of a Coke bottle with the trademark "Napalm."[150] One urges resistance with the text "The Law Requires that You Inform Your Draft Board of All

FIGURE 42   "USA Terror." Rome, June 2004.
Photograph by the author.

Changes in Status, Obey the Law to the Letter, Jam Your Board May 1970"; a raised
fist clutches a bundle of letters over the Greek letter Omega (Ω), a symbol of the
anti-draft movement during the Vietnam War.

   We cannot conclude that the posters provide us with a direct line to the politics
of the artists. The posters are rhetorical, which means that they are crafted to present variations on traditional and emerging vernacular commonplaces of the political and the visual that were already at large in the debate about the war. Because the
posters are evidently rhetorical, we must presume that they are not simply testimo-
nials or expressions of opinion; they are, rather, appeals—visual arguments crafted
to be addressed to viewers who might agree, be won over, or mobilized. Further, the

FIGURE 43   "Fuck Bush." Rome, June 2004.
Photograph by the author.

posters are not only addressed to viewers but offered to others for their own persuasive uses. The artists of these posters, some of whom might in fact have gone
on to become graphic designers working for clients selling soap or cars, were
designing posters for prospective "clients," who might display the posters on their
own walls, windows, and fences. In some cases, at least, the posters were literally
made, with donated labor and materials, for clients for whom the artists produced
posters announcing various events taking place on and around campus. It
appears that at least some of the posters were produced by the artists at the
request of the strike leaders. A poster in the UC Archives bearing the text "Unite"
shows a yin-yang circle; in one cell is a raised fist, in the other a raised hand making the peace gesture. But in another poster in the archives, the "V" peace gesture
is replaced in the centered yin-yang circle by a hand with a raised middle finger.

FIGURE 44   "USA Terror," with figure from Abu
Ghraib photo. Rome, June 2004. Photograph by
the author.

In pen, handwritten, are the words "To the Management: We are all proletarians
here. We do not have a fancy 24-hour staff and plush offices. Next time you bureaucrats want something done by 8:00, either donate your own manpower or get your
order in at 10:00 P.M. like everyone else, preferably both." Then, at the bottom of
the poster, in ink, "Love, The Movement." Apparently the "bureaucrats" referred to
are the student strike leaders, who had asked for a rush job of a batch of posters.[151]

There are interpretive hazards in trying to identify any central tendency in the
posters. Because viewers and users seldom saw all of the posters, the rhetorical
experience of the posters was diffused and various, both materially and politically.
Still, perhaps it is not merely sentimental to argue that the posters as a whole, in all
their political variety, demonstrate a commitment to civic discourse that contrasts
with the experiences of Paris in May 1968. In the Atelier Populaire, posters were

FIGURE 45   "USA Terror." Rome, June 2004.
Photograph by the author.

proposed to the group, which voted its approval, declining, we are told, to produce
orthodox Marxist propaganda. In Berkeley, the general project seems directed at a
public that is called to take citizen action. And yet more radical appeals are also part
of the mix, indicating not a parliamentary dialogue, exactly—after all, these are
posters, not speeches—and yet more than a sixties "do your own thing" mentality.
If such a view is correct, even those few radical posters may be regarded as part of
a practice that celebrated core civic values. The client is peace.

    If the posters were "liberal" and "democratic," in the sense that they were mod-
erate, procedural, humanist, and civic, it may well be that they were unrepresenta-
tive of the most extreme SDS followers and of the Cold War liberals who supported
the war, and of their alleged successor, an exhausted liberalism that, according to
historian David Burner, came next—a liberalism of identity politics and preoccu-
pation with the self that after 1970 undermined the capacity of New Deal–style

FIGURE 46   "No Blood for Oil." Rome, June 2004.
Photograph by the author.

liberalism to build coalitions among groups, classes, and interests to serve the collective good.[152] The posters themselves recall ideologically the origins of student
political reawakenings in the early 1960s, when young people began asking in
earnest for society to enact the ideals of civil liberties, racial justice, and peace
professed by their parents, asserting a hope for democratic and progressive action
for peace. They form a micro-chapter in the history of images in the twentieth
century that, according to Robert Hariman and John Louis Lucaites, continually
rebalances liberal individualism and the mutual obligations of democratic citizenship. Hariman and Lucaites write that "the icons of U.S. public culture
increasingly underwrite liberalism more than they do democracy, and we believe
this imbalance threatens progressive social and economic policies and ultimately
democracy itself."[153]

FIGURE 47   "No Blood for Oil!" Hand sprayed.
Also showing "Stop Wars" stencil. Rome, June
2004. Photograph by the author.

The Berkeley posters cluster around the core concerns of the student movements and the politics of the 1960s—civil liberties, racial justice, peace—and are
overwhelmingly focused on the Vietnam War as a historical contingency and a
moral imperative.

It may be that the posters reveal less about the politics of the artists than the
politics of the audiences to whom the posters were addressed—sympathetic liberals at the university and in the community. In any case, the posters were clearly an
effort to construct and motivate a public focused on ending the war by asserting the
centrality and patriotism of peace and civic dissent.

The Berkeley peace posters were apparently made mostly by students, with support and encouragement from some faculty. It seems certain that some of the posters circulated from Wurster Hall were brought in from outside, from the student
poster workshops in San Francisco or at Stanford University and elsewhere. But

FIGURE 48   "Wanted [Bush]." Rome, June 2004.
Photograph by the author.

though they are student works, the posters do not on the surface appear to take a
strictly "student" point of view, whatever that might be. They do not mostly display
the militant and doctrinaire mirror-image politics that, according to Kevin Moist,
the core of the hippie culture attributed to student radicalism. Nor do the posters
whine about school. Some of the posters' subjects are students—most evidently in
the posters about the killings at Kent State and Jackson State—but the posters do
not articulate a complaint or a rebellion against university authorities, or against
school in general, as some student protest of the time was accused of doing and to
some extent did. John le Carré catches the flavor of these strains of youthful unhap-
piness and confused politics in his depiction of a young actress, Charlie, who is the
protagonist of *The Little Drummer Girl*. The Israeli agent who recruits Charlie for
an infiltration prepares himself for her: "At the hard end, he had Fanon, Guevara,
and Marighella; at the soft, Debray, Sartre, and Marcuse; not to mention the gentler
souls who wrote mainly of the cruelties of education in consumerist societies, the
horrors of religion, and the fatal cramping of the spirit in capitalist childhood."[154]

FIGURE 49 "USA Terror." Stencils on sidewalk.
Rome, June 2004. Photograph by the author.

Bryan Turner recalls his own reluctance, while a graduate student in sociology at Leeds, to follow the Paris protests of May 1968, which he saw as narcissistic and impractical: "I was deeply unimpressed by the student revolt. . . . At the time, I thought there were deep social inequalities between social classes that required radical economic and political solutions involving a systematic redistribution of resources rather than critique of bureaucratic authority in public institutions such as universities."[155]

In contrast to the strains of juvenile romanticism that Moist, le Carré, and Turner attribute to student protests of the time, or to the radical fragmentation and collapse described by Tom Hayden, Todd Gitlin, and Kirkpatrick Sale, the Berkeley posters typically appeal for moral concern about war and peace, and they call for civic engagement, mostly avoiding revolutionary romanticism, student-centered complaints, and factional dogmatism.

The Berkeley posters, modest and ephemeral as they are, are perhaps worth remembering for their call for maturity—their insistence that peace is patriotic—rather than for any sort of childish incivility or romantic violence.

FIGURE 50   Peace demonstration. Montpelier,
Vermont, July 2005. Photograph by the author.

One sees a similar tone in the more muted protests against America's war in
Iraq during the administration of President George W. Bush. In figure 50, at about
the same time the Rome graffiti were appearing, is the scene in a small state capi-
tal, Montpelier, Vermont, where a few respectable citizens, perhaps former Berkeley students settled into middle age, are keeping up the cause. Perhaps two of those
Berkeley students from 1970 settled into suburban central Pennsylvania, where in
the winter of 2008 they longed for a presidential candidate of whatever party to
bring peace (see fig. 51).

At Berkeley, the tradition of protest has continued. In the aftermath of the Great
Recession of 2008 and cascading budget cuts in California, tuition rose rapidly at
the University of California, sparking student protests. On the Berkeley campus in
November 2010, the sun was shining on Sproul Plaza, the scene of the Free Speech
Movement and countless political demonstrations (see fig. 52). On this November
noon, a rally was in progress for an upcoming football game. Around campus,
posters hung by the administration advertised the happiness of Berkeley students
(see fig. 53). At the plaza of Dwinelle Hall, just off Sproul Plaza, a student protest
against tuition increases was under way, with demonstrators directly quoting and
mocking the university advertising posters (see fig. 54).

FIGURE 51   Yard signs for Ron Paul and Dennis
Kucinich. Central Pennsylvania, early 2008. The
sign on the mailbox reads, "Endless War," on
which "less" is crossed out and replaced with
"this." Photograph by the author.

In November 2011, on the campus at Berkeley, police armed with clubs attacked
nonviolent students and professors who were part of the Occupy Wall Street movement; students at UC Davis were pepper sprayed by campus police.[156]

The Berkeley posters were made by hand, designed by student artists, and circulated locally. They survive in a few archives and perhaps a few attics. In the early
twenty-first century, posters can be designed on a laptop using ready-made tem-
plates in word processing software, or by using more sophisticated desktop photography and design software with automated "posterize" filters. Handheld tablet
computers have apps that turn a photograph into a poster by reducing the color palette and allowing for the insertion of captions and text boxes. The resulting posters,

FIGURE 52   Football rally, Sproul Plaza.
University of California, Berkeley. November 2010.
Photograph by the author.

whether created by amateurs or professionals, can be circulated worldwide in sec-
onds over Internet social media sites. Such was the case with the original Adbusters
poster for the Occupy Wall Street movement, which called for an occupation of
Wall Street on September 17, 2011. The poster shows a ballerina standing on the
back of a charging bronze Wall Street bull; shadowy figures in the background
appear ready for a fight. The Occupy and the Tea Party movements have produced
hundreds of posters. Poster design is still taught as part of the curriculum for
graphic designers, and posters continue to be produced for museums, events, colleges, and dormitory rooms.

     The posters in the 1970 collection call for nonviolent political participation, for
belief, for feeling, and for identification with an assertive and peaceful civic identity.
To be sure, the antiwar protests of the period, at Berkeley and elsewhere, were not
always so peaceful. At the demonstrations in Berkeley, I remember seeing a junior
high school boy carried away by the drama of the moment, winging a tear gas grenade back down the street at a group of Alameda County deputies in their blue riot
gear (they were widely called the Blue Meanies).[157] A small wing of the SDS became

FIGURE 53 Poster in Dwinelle Plaza.
University of California, Berkeley, November 2010.
Photograph by the author.

FIGURE 54   Student tuition protest. University of
California, Berkeley, November 2010. Photograph
by the author.

increasingly carried away with fantasies of revolutionary violence, and some did
turn to arson, rioting, bombs, and guns. Mostly, however, the antiwar movement
was a sporadic and peaceful affair.

The struggle for the memory of the long 1960s continues, producing continuing histories and memoirs in which the temptations to sensationalize or sentimen-
talize are strong. The Berkeley posters of May 1970 have a strong claim to be part
of the public memory of those times.

In the little world of speech communication and rhetorical studies, the times
were changing, too, in ways that were partly influenced by the Vietnam War and the
civil rights movement, by student protest and civil disorder. Scholars began to map
the rhetorical dimensions of non-oratorical rhetoric, or to warn that such effusions
were not, in principle, rhetoric at all. Early in May 1970, in the midst of the national

confusion, a small group of rhetorical scholars was called together to consider the prospects of rhetoric. They met as part of the National Developmental Project on Rhetoric, directed by Lloyd Bitzer and Edwin Black of the University of Wisconsin, supported by a grant from the National Endowment for the Humanities and the Speech Communication Association. The project met in two stages. The first was a conference at the Wingspread Conference Center in Racine, Wisconsin, where a dozen scholars presented papers that had been commissioned as part of the project. The second half of the conference met at the Pheasant Run conference center in St. Charles, Illinois, May 10–15, 1970. At the Pheasant Run conference, twenty-three scholars (as at the Wingspread conference, all the conferees were men) met to "refine, amplify, and translate the Wingspread ideas into recommendations . . . related to the humanistic study of rhetorical communication."[158]

I was one of the twenty-three who met at Pheasant Run, where we were divided into three committees—on rhetorical criticism, on the scope of rhetoric, and on rhetorical invention.[159] The conferees had all come from campuses marked in various ways by a decade of political turmoil, and at the very least they shared the view that rhetorical scholarship might have something to contribute to an understanding of what was happening to the country, both by unmasking the rhetoric of power and by recovering academically marginalized rhetorics of peace and civil rights in various genres and media.

In the decade before Pheasant Run, the discipline had paid increasing attention to the rhetoric of protest, of literature, and of a variety of visual media, but many scholars still resisted such an enlargement of the rhetorical agenda on the grounds that rhetorical scholarship was not fitted for such work or, more sweepingly, that rhetoric itself could properly occur only in verbal persuasion. In this view, whatever else they might be, images (or fiction, or poetry, or demonstrations) were not rhetoric. Gatekeepers were sometimes, but not always, satisfied with an appeal to the much-cited passage in Aristotle's *Rhetoric*, perhaps seized out of context, to justify the study of "the available means of persuasion." Much of the resistance to the opening of rhetorical studies was put to rest by the report of the National Developmental Project on Rhetoric, which issued *The Prospect of Rhetoric* in 1971. The project's committee on the scope of rhetoric and its place in higher education explicitly encouraged the study of "theory and practice of forms of communication which have not been as thoroughly investigated as public address"; its committee on rhetorical criticism asserted that "rhetorical criticism may be applied to any human act, process, product or artifact which, in the critic's view, may formulate, sustain, or modify attention, perceptions, attitudes, or behavior."[160] *The Prospect of Rhetoric* did not actually call into being the increasing attention to visual rhetoric, but the report did reassure the gatekeepers that such work was legitimately part of rhetorical studies, and it was often cited in journal essays to accomplish just such a purpose.[161]

At the end of the week the Pheasant Run conferees returned to homes and campuses. In Berkeley, demonstrations and the "On Strike—Keep It Open" movement continued, and posters continued to appear.

Rhetorical scholarship has grown in scope and depth in the years since the events of May 1970. Interdisciplinary scholars in visual rhetoric have refounded the study of visual rhetoric and have participated in creating a multidisciplinary field of visual rhetoric. Rhetorical and communication scholars have deepened and broadened the study of visual rhetoric and its interdisciplinary connections with other fields, and have done so without creating the fragmentation of the discipline that was sometimes feared by those who witnessed the beginnings of this line of work. They have done this without abandoning the long tradition of discursive civic rhetoric; nor have they presumed that all the visual images they study are reducible to a discursive paraphrase or civic gesture. In their theorizing and critical analysis, they have reshaped the entire discipline and have reached out to other disciplines. It is their work that the conferees at Pheasant Run dreamed of.

The war, of course, dragged on. Richard Nixon easily won reelection against George McGovern, who ran as a peace candidate in 1972. Then came the unfolding of Watergate, the resignation in scandal of Vice President Agnew, the resignation of President Nixon, the arrivals of Gerald Ford, Jimmy Carter, and Ronald Reagan. Peace, or at least a sort of resolution, finally came in Vietnam—partly because of reverses on the field of battle; the consequent abandonment by the press of the ongoing slaughter in Southeast Asia; the firmness and integrity of a small and growing minority of both parties in Congress; the efforts of presidential candidates who were willing to court defeat at the polls to make the case against the war; the work of historians, journalists, political scientists, and others who taught the attentive fraction of the country about the war; and numerous other contingencies that went far beyond the work of a few anonymous graphic artists in Berkeley, California, in May 1970. But those student protesters and artists played their parts.

THE BERKELEY PEACE POSTERS

in the Penn State University Collection

PLATES

1] "Does He Destroy Your Way of Life?"
Thomas W. Benson Political Protest Collection,
Historical Collections and Labor Archives, Eberly
Family Special Collections Library, University
Libraries, The Pennsylvania State University. Box
1, Folder 2. 14 × 12 in.

2] "Nature Is Beautiful (So Is Human Nature)
Conserve It." Berkeley, California, 1970. Thomas
W. Benson Political Protest Collection, Historical
Collections and Labor Archives, Eberly Family
Special Collections Library, University Libraries,
The Pennsylvania State University. Box 1, Folder
14. 15 × 11 in.

3] "This Is Life—This Cuts It Short." Berkeley,
California, 1970. Thomas W. Benson Political Pro-
test Collection, Historical Collections and Labor
Archives, Eberly Family Special Collections
Library, University Libraries, The Pennsylvania
State University. Box 1, Folder 14. 15 × 11 in.

4] "Vietnamization." Berkeley, California,
1970. Thomas W. Benson Political Protest Collection, Historical Collections and Labor Archives,
Eberly Family Special Collections Library, University Libraries, The Pennsylvania State University.
Box 1, Folder 4. 12.25 × 18 in.

5] "It Became Necessary to Destroy the Town
to Save It." Berkeley, California, 1970. Thomas W.
Benson Political Protest Collection, Historical Collections and Labor Archives, Eberly Family Special
Collections Library, University Libraries, The Pennsylvania State University. Box 1, Folder 4. 18 ×
12.25 in.

6] "Free Asia—U.S. Get Out Now." Berkeley, Cal-
ifornia, 1970. Thomas W. Benson Political Protest
Collection, Historical Collections and Labor
Archives, Eberly Family Special Collections Library,
University Libraries, The Pennsylvania State Univer-
sity. Box 1, Folder 10. 15 × 22 in.

7] "Asia for Asians!!" Berkeley, California, 1970.
Thomas W. Benson Political Protest Collection, Historical Collections and Labor Archives, Eberly Family Special Collections Library, University Libraries,
The Pennsylvania State University. Box 1, Folder 17.
33 × 15 in.

8] "Her Suffering for Our Comfort? STRIKE."
Berkeley, California, 1970. Thomas W. Benson Polit-
ical Protest Collection, Historical Collections and
Labor Archives, Eberly Family Special Collections
Library, University Libraries, The Pennsylvania State
University. Box 1, Folder 12. 22 × 15 in.

9] "Kent State University. May 4th, 1970."
Berkeley, California, 1970. Thomas W. Benson Polit-
ical Protest Collection, Historical Collections and
Labor Archives, Eberly Family Special Collections
Library, University Libraries, The Pennsylvania State
University. Box 1, Folder 4. 12.25 × 19 in.

10] "Kent State. Augusta, Georgia." Berkeley,
California, 1970. Thomas W. Benson Political Pro-
test Collection, Historical Collections and Labor
Archives, Eberly Family Special Collections Library,
University Libraries, The Pennsylvania State Univer-
sity. Box 1, Folder 10. 22 × 15 in.

11] "All His Parents' Love and Devotion Did Not
Save the Life of This Boy." Berkeley, California,
1970. Thomas W. Benson Political Protest Collec-
tion, Historical Collections and Labor Archives,
Eberly Family Special Collections Library, University
Libraries, The Pennsylvania State University. Box 1,
Folder 7. 22.5 × 17.5 in.

12] "Amerika Is Devouring Its Children." Jay Belloli. Berkeley, California, 1970. Thomas W. Benson Political Protest Collection, Historical Collections and Labor Archives, Eberly Family Special Collections Library, University Libraries, The Pennsylvania State University. Box 1, Folder 13. 22 × 15 in.

13] "Did You Vote for This? Who Did?" Berkeley, California, 1970. Thomas W. Benson Political Protest Collection, Historical Collections and Labor Archives, Eberly Family Special Collections Library, University Libraries, The Pennsylvania State University. Box 1, Folder 11. 22 × 15 in.

14] "Security Is a Silent Majority." Berkeley, California, 1970. Thomas W. Benson Political Protest Collection, Historical Collections and Labor Archives, Eberly Family Special Collections Library, University Libraries, The Pennsylvania State University. Box 1, Folder 5. 15 × 11 in.

15] "Big Brother Is Watching You. So Do Something." Thomas W. Benson Political Protest Collection, Historical Collections and Labor Archives, Eberly Family Special Collections Library, University Libraries, The Pennsylvania State University. Box 1, Folder 5. 13 × 11 in.

16] [Hitler with mask of Nixon.] Thomas W. Benson Political Protest Collection, Historical Collections and Labor Archives, Eberly Family Special Collections Library, University Libraries, The Pennsylvania State University. Box 1, Folder 23. 32.5 × 28 in.

17] "An Effete Corps of Impudent Snobs." Thomas W. Benson Political Protest Collection, Historical Collections and Labor Archives, Eberly Family Special Collections Library, University Libraries, The Pennsylvania State University. Box 1, Folder 7. 24 × 18 in.

18] "Run This One Up Your Flagpole, Dick!" Thomas W. Benson Political Protest Collection, Historical Collections and Labor Archives, Eberly Family Special Collections Library, University Libraries, The Pennsylvania State University. Box 1, Folder 8. 22 × 14 in.

19] "Recycle Nixon." Thomas W. Benson Political Protest Collection, Historical Collections and Labor Archives, Eberly Family Special Collections Library, University Libraries, The Pennsylvania State University. Box 1, Folder 13. 15 × 22 in.

20] "No Nixon Agnew War." Thomas W. Benson Political Protest Collection, Historical Collections and Labor Archives, Eberly Family Special Collections Library, University Libraries, The Pennsylvania State University. Box 1, Folder 22. 24 × 17.75 in.

21] "Money Talks—Boycott War Profiteers." Thomas W. Benson Political Protest Collection, Historical Collections and Labor Archives, Eberly Family Special Collections Library, University Libraries, The Pennsylvania State University. Box 1, Folder 7. 23 × 14 in.

22] "Boycott War. Buy Peace." Thomas W. Benson Political Protest Collection, Historical Collections and Labor Archives, Eberly Family Special Collections Library, University Libraries, The Pennsylvania State University.

23] "Peace Now." Thomas W. Benson Political Protest Collection, Historical Collections and Labor Archives, Eberly Family Special Collections Library, University Libraries, The Pennsylvania State University. Box 1, Folder 23. 28.5 × 23 in.

24] "War Kills." Thomas W. Benson Political Protest Collection, Historical Collections and Labor Archives, Eberly Family Special Collections Library, University Libraries, The Pennsylvania State University. Box 1, Folder 8. 22 × 14 in.

25] "Up Against the War Motherland." Thomas W. Benson Political Protest Collection, Historical Collections and Labor Archives, Eberly Family Special Collections Library, University Libraries, The Pennsylvania State University. Box 1, Folder 13. 22 × 15 in.

26] "War Is Unhealthy for America." Thomas W. Benson Political Protest Collection, Historical Collections and Labor Archives, Eberly Family Special Collections Library, University Libraries, The Pennsylvania State University. Box 1, Folder 12. 15 × 22 in.

27] "It's Only the Beginning." Thomas W. Benson Political Protest Collection, Historical Collections and Labor Archives, Eberly Family Special Collections Library, University Libraries, The Pennsylvania State University. Box 1, Folder 23. 28.5 × 23 in.

28] "Let There Be Peace and Let It Begin With Me." Thomas W. Benson Political Protest Collection, Historical Collections and Labor Archives, Eberly Family Special Collections Library, University Libraries, The Pennsylvania State University. Box 1, Folder 23. 23 × 28 in.

29] "Peace Now." Thomas W. Benson Political Protest Collection, Historical Collections and Labor Archives, Eberly Family Special Collections Library, University Libraries, The Pennsylvania State University. Box 1, Folder 12. 22 × 15 in.

30] "Vietnam: Spilled Blood Split the Country." Thomas W. Benson Political Protest Collection, Historical Collections and Labor Archives, Eberly Family Special Collections Library, University Libraries, The Pennsylvania State University. Box 1, Folder 23. 29 × 23 in.

31] "Stop War." Thomas W. Benson Political Protest Collection, Historical Collections and Labor Archives, Eberly Family Special Collections Library, University Libraries, The Pennsylvania State University. Box 1, Folder 23. 34 × 22.5 in.

32] "Yes on Peace." Thomas W. Benson Political Protest Collection, Historical Collections and Labor Archives, Eberly Family Special Collections Library, University Libraries, The Pennsylvania State University. Box 1, Folder 17. 22 × 15 in.

33] "Unity in Our Love of Man." Thomas W. Benson Political Protest Collection, Historical Collections and Labor Archives, Eberly Family Special Collections Library, University Libraries, The Pennsylvania State University. Box 1, Folder 13. 22 × 15 in.

34] "Home for Peace." Thomas W. Benson Political Protest Collection, Historical Collections and Labor Archives, Eberly Family Special Collections Library, University Libraries, The Pennsylvania State University. Box 1, Folder 3. 22 × 8 in.

35] "Peace Is Patriotic." Thomas W. Benson Political Protest Collection, Historical Collections and Labor Archives, Eberly Family Special Collections Library, University Libraries, The Pennsylvania State University. Box 1, Folder 5. 22 × 15 in.

36] "Peace Now." Thomas W. Benson Political Protest Collection, Historical Collections and Labor Archives, Eberly Family Special Collections Library, University Libraries, The Pennsylvania State University. Box 1, Folder 15. 22 × 15 in.

37] "Lets Have Peace. Lisa." Thomas W. Benson Political Protest Collection, Historical Collections and Labor Archives, Eberly Family Special Collections Library, University Libraries, The Pennsylvania State University. Box 1, Folder 11. 22 × 15 in.

38] "Peace." Thomas W. Benson Political Protest Collection, Historical Collections and Labor Archives, Eberly Family Special Collections Library, University Libraries, The Pennsylvania State University. Box 1, Folder 12. 33 × 15 in.

39] "Peace This Year." Thomas W. Benson Political Protest Collection, Historical Collections and Labor Archives, Eberly Family Special Collections Library, University Libraries, The Pennsylvania State University. Box 1, Folder 15. 15 × 33 in.

40] "Americans Want Peace." Thomas W. Benson Political Protest Collection, Historical Collections and Labor Archives, Eberly Family Special Collections Library, University Libraries, The Pennsylvania State University. Box 1, Folder 16. 22 × 15 in.

41] "Come Together for Peace." Thomas W. Benson Political Protest Collection, Historical Collections and Labor Archives, Eberly Family Special Collections Library, University Libraries, The Pennsylvania State University. Box 1, Folder 5. 11 × 15 in.

42] "Unite for Peace." Thomas W. Benson Political Protest Collection, Historical Collections and Labor Archives, Eberly Family Special Collections Library, University Libraries, The Pennsylvania State University. Box 1, Folder 23. 23.75 × 31.5 in.

43] "Remember When Life Was Simple?" Thomas W. Benson Political Protest Collection, Historical Collections and Labor Archives, Eberly Family Special Collections Library, University Libraries, The Pennsylvania State University. Box 1, Folder 5. 11 × 15 in.

44] [American flag with rifles and airplanes.] Thomas W. Benson Political Protest Collection, Historical Collections and Labor Archives, Eberly Family Special Collections Library, University Libraries, The Pennsylvania State University. Box 1, Folder 8. 22 × 14 in.

45] "Peace Now." Thomas W. Benson Political Protest Collection, Historical Collections and Labor Archives, Eberly Family Special Collections Library, University Libraries, The Pennsylvania State University. Box 1, Folder 22. 24 × 17.75 in.

46] "America Saves the World." Thomas W. Benson Political Protest Collection, Historical Collections and Labor Archives, Eberly Family Special Collections Library, University Libraries, The Pennsylvania State University. Box 1, Folder 7. 18 × 24 in.

47] "Did We Really Come in Peace for All Mankind?" Thomas W. Benson Political Protest Collection, Historical Collections and Labor Archives, Eberly Family Special Collections Library, University Libraries, The Pennsylvania State University. Box 1, Folder 10. 14 × 22 in.

48] "End War Now." Thomas W. Benson Political Protest Collection, Historical Collections and Labor Archives, Eberly Family Special Collections Library, University Libraries, The Pennsylvania State University. Box 1, Folder 22. 24 × 17.75 in.

49] "Remember Peace? Speak Out to End War." Thomas W. Benson Political Protest Collection, Historical Collections and Labor Archives, Eberly Family Special Collections Library, University Libraries, The Pennsylvania State University. Box 1, Folder 23. 30.5 × 22 in.

50] "Washington!" Thomas W. Benson Political Protest Collection, Historical Collections and Labor Archives, Eberly Family Special Collections Library, University Libraries, The Pennsylvania State University. Box 1, Folder 20. 33.75 × 30 in.

51] "The Fall Offensive Against the War in Vietnam. March November 15" [1969]. Thomas W. Benson Political Protest Collection, Historical Collections and Labor Archives, Eberly Family Special Collections Library, University Libraries, The Pennsylvania State University. Box 1, Folder 20. 20 × 12.5 in.

52] "Unite Against the War." Thomas W. Benson Political Protest Collection, Historical Collections and Labor Archives, Eberly Family Special Collections Library, University Libraries, The Pennsylvania State University. Box 1, Folder 17. 33 × 15 in.

53] "Seize the Time." Thomas W. Benson Political Protest Collection, Historical Collections and Labor Archives, Eberly Family Special Collections Library, University Libraries, The Pennsylvania State University. Box 1, Folder 8. 22 × 15 in.

54] "Free All Political Prisoners." Thomas W. Benson Political Protest Collection, Historical Collections and Labor Archives, Eberly Family Special Collections Library, University Libraries, The Pennsylvania State University. Box 1, Folder 15. 22 × 15 in.

55] "America When Will You Be Angelic? . . ." Thomas W. Benson Political Protest Collection, Historical Collections and Labor Archives, Eberly Family Special Collections Library, University Libraries, The Pennsylvania State University. Box 1, Folder 15. 22 × 15 in.

56] "War Alarm . . . Ban the Bomb! . . ." Thomas W. Benson Political Protest Collection, Historical Collections and Labor Archives, Eberly Family Special Collections Library, University Libraries, The Pennsylvania State University. Box 1, Folder 9. 22 × 14 in.

57] "Write for Peace." Thomas W. Benson Political Protest Collection, Historical Collections and Labor Archives, Eberly Family Special Collections Library, University Libraries, The Pennsylvania State University. Box 1, Folder 12. 15 × 22 in.

58] "Speak Out, You Got to Speak Out Against the Madness, You Got to Speak Your Mind." Thomas W. Benson Political Protest Collection, Historical Collections and Labor Archives, Eberly Family Special Collections Library, University Libraries, The Pennsylvania State University. Box 1, Folder 17. 15 × 22 in.

59] "He Didn't Protest Either." Thomas W. Benson Political Protest Collection, Historical Collections and Labor Archives, Eberly Family Special Collections Library, University Libraries, The Pennsylvania State University. Box 1, Folder 17. 22 × 15 in.

60] "Don't Be a Silent Part of the War Machine. Speak Out Against Cambodia." Thomas W. Benson Political Protest Collection, Historical Collections and Labor Archives, Eberly Family Special Collections Library, University Libraries, The Pennsylvania State University. Box 1, Folder 11. 22 × 15 in.

61] "America Is a Democracy Only as Long as It Represents the Will of the People." Thomas W. Benson Political Protest Collection, Historical Collections and Labor Archives, Eberly Family Special Collections Library, University Libraries, The Pennsylvania State University. Box 1, Folder 6. 22.5 × 17.5 in.

62] "You Are Already Involved." Thomas W. Benson Political Protest Collection, Historical Collections and Labor Archives, Eberly Family Special Collections Library, University Libraries, The Pennsylvania State University. Box 1, Folder 6. 21.5 × 17.5 in.

63] "America Says: Actions Speak Louder than Words." Thomas W. Benson Political Protest Collection, Historical Collections and Labor Archives, Eberly Family Special Collections Library, University Libraries, The Pennsylvania State University. Box 1, Folder 6. 17 × 11 in.

64] "Don't Be 1 of the Silent Majority—Speak Out." Thomas W. Benson Political Protest Collection, Historical Collections and Labor Archives, Eberly Family Special Collections Library, University Libraries, The Pennsylvania State University. Box 1, Folder 14. 22 × 15 in.

65] "Join Now." Thomas W. Benson Political Protest Collection, Historical Collections and Labor Archives, Eberly Family Special Collections Library, University Libraries, The Pennsylvania State University. Box 1, Folder 21. 24 × 17.5 in.

66] "Speak Out Against the War." Thomas W. Benson Political Protest Collection, Historical Collections and Labor Archives, Eberly Family Special Collections Library, University Libraries, The Pennsylvania State University. Box 1, Folder 21. 24 × 17.5 in.

PLATE 1

PLATE 2

PLATE 3

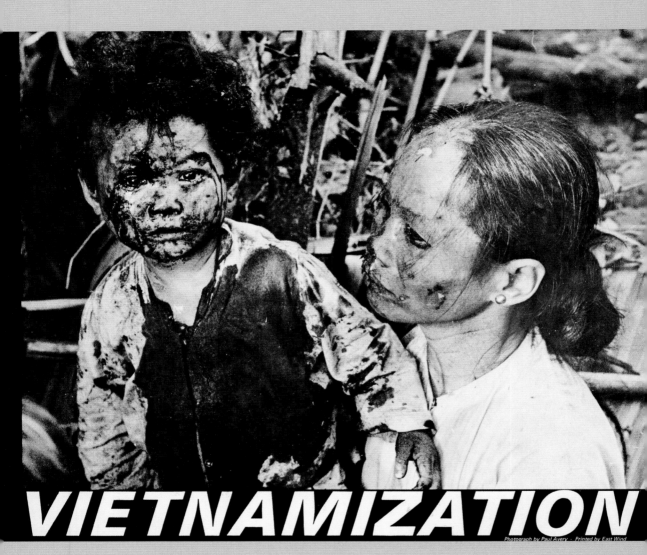

VIETNAMIZATION

Photograph by Paul Avery · Printed by East Wind

PLATE 4

"It became necessary to destroy the town to save it."

— unidentified U.S. Army Major quoted by Associated Press Correspondent Peter Arnett in newspapers of February 7, 1968. The Major was referring to the destruction of the town of Ben Tre which had been overrun by a regimental-size force (approx. 2500 troops) of Viet Cong. Ben Tre had a civilian population of about 35,000. The fight to wrest Ben Tre from Viet Cong control cost the lives of an estimated 1000 civilians.

Photograph by Paul Avery · Printed by East Wind

PLATE 5

PLATE 6

PLATE 7

PLATE 8

KENT STATE
UNIVERSITY
MAY 4th, 1970

PLATE 9

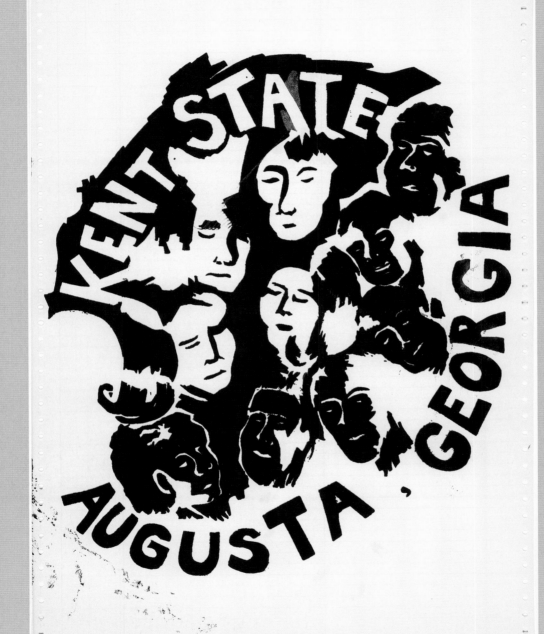

PLATE 10

JEFFREY MILLER, KILLED MAY, 1970, KENT STATE UNIVERSITY, OHIO

All his parents' love and devotion did not save the life of the this boy.
YOU can help save the lives of others.

WORK FOR PEACE !!
THINGS YOU CAN DO:

1. Send letters, telegrams, or petitions to: President Nixon; Senator Alan Cranston; Senator George Murphy; Representative William Maillard; Representative Philip Burton; Representative Jeffrey Cohelan; Senator William Fulbright (Chairman Senate Foreign Relations Committee); Senators Mark Hatfield and Charles Goodell (supporting their bills to withhold any military appropriations for the war in Southeast Asia beyond December 31, 1970 except for troop withdrawal); Representative George Brown (motion to impeach President Nixon for violating the

United States Constitution); Representatives Kastemier, Kock, Ottinger, and Tunney and Senator Young (resolution to censure President Nixon).
2. Start an economic boycott by restricting your purchases to necessary food and living expenses.
3. If you have Savings Bonds, sell them. If you are on the Payroll Savings Plan, withdraw from it. Besides being a poor investment, these bonds help underwrite the war.
4. Do not pay your telephone tax. It was put on specifically to help pay for the war in Vietnam. Your phone will not be cut off.

5. Get your church to take a stand against the expansion of the war and communicate this stand to the press and to Washington.
6. Introduce resolutions into every organization you belong to, getting them to go on record against the war. Get them to send a representative to Washington to lobby with others who are coming in from all over the country. Get your group to express its stand to the Board of Supervisors or City Council.
7. Go to your union meeting and get this resolution passed.

8. Wear a black armband.
9. Get together with some friends and buy a spot announcement on the radio indicating your opposition to the war.
10. Send a letter to all the magazines and newspapers to which you subscribe.
11. Call in to a radio talk show.
12. Talk to your neighbors and encourage them to do some of these activities.
13. Think up your own ideas and pass them on.

KAMKAZI DESIGN GROUP

PLATE 11

PLATE 12

DID YOU VOTE FOR THIS ?

WHO DID ?

PLATE 13

PLATE 14

PLATE 15

PLATE 16

PLATE 17

PLATE 18

PLATE 19

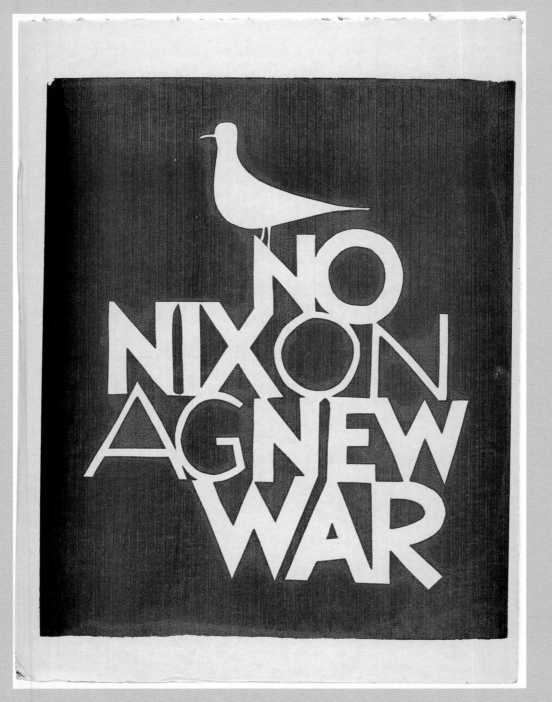

PLATE 20

MONEY TALKS

BOYCOTT WAR PROFITEERS

PLATE 21

PLATE 22

PLATE 23

PLATE 24

UP AGAINST THE WAR MOTHERLAND

4973

PLATE 25

PLATE 26

PLATE 27

LET THERE BE PEACE AND LET IT BEGIN WITH ME

PLATE 28

PLATE 29

PLATE 30

PLATE 31

PLATE 32

497ᵗ

PLATE 33

PLATE 34

PLATE 35

PLATE 36

PLATE 37

PLATE 38

PLATE 39

4973

PLATE 40

PLATE 41

UNITE
FOR
PEACE

PLATE 42

PLATE 43

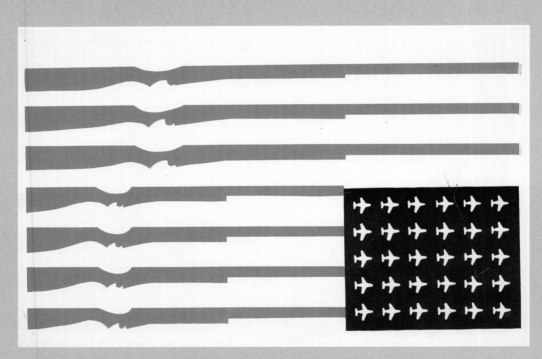

PLATE 44

PLATE 45

PLATE 46

DID
WE
REALLY
COME
IN
PEACE
FOR
ALL
MANKIND?

PLATE 47

PLATE 48

REMBMBER PEACE?
SPEAK OUT
TO END WAR

PLATE 49

PLATE 50

THE FALL OFFENSIVE AGAINST THE WAR IN VIETNAM

MARCH
NOVEMBER 15

SAN FRANCISCO   NEW MOBE - BAY PAC
2170 Bryant · 285-8660

LABOR DONATED

PLATE 51

PLATE 52

PLATE 53

PLATE 54

PLATE 55

"War Alarm.. Ban The Bomb!
In Every City...
On Every Farm.
Stop The War in Viet Nam...
Freedom Now To Alabam'...
It's Zero Hour Sister,
It's Zero Hour Brother...
We've Got To Hurry,
To Save One Another."

TOM ROBERTS

PLATE 56

Write for Peace

RAPE

PLATE 57

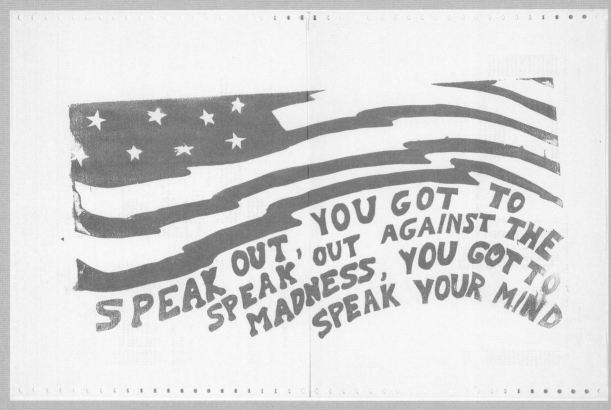

PLATE 58

PLATE 59

Don't Be a Silent
of The War Part
Machine

SPeak OUT
against cambodia

PLATE 60

AMERICA IS A DEMOCRACY
ONLY AS LONG AS IT REPRESENTS THE WILL OF THE PEOPLE.

UNITE FOR PEACE!!
THINGS <u>YOU</u> CAN DO:

1. Send letters, telegrams, or petitions to: President Nixon; Senator Alan Cranston; Senator George Murphy; Representative William Maillard; Representative Philip Burton; Representative Jeffrey Cohelan; Senator William Fulbright (Chairman Senate Foreign Relations Committee); Senators Mark Hatfield and Charles Goodell (supporting their bills to withhold any military appropriations for the war in Southeast Asia beyond December 31, 1970 except for troop withdrawal); Representative George Brown (motion to impeach President Nixon for violating the

United States Constitution); Representatives Kastemier, Kock, Ottinger, and Tunney and Senator Young (resolution to censure President Nixon).
2. Start an economic boycott by restricting your purchases to necessary food and living expenses.
3. If you have Savings Bonds, sell them. If you are on the Payroll Savings Plan, withdraw from it. Besides being a poor investment, these bonds help underwrite the war.
4. Do not pay your telephone tax. It was put on specifically to help pay for the war in Vietnam. Your phone will not be cut off.

5. Get your church to take a stand against the expansion of the war and communicate this stand to the press and to Washington.
6. Introduce resolutions into every organization you belong to, getting them to go on record against the war. Get them to send a representative to Washington to lobby with others who are coming in from all over the country. Get your group to express its stand to the Board of Supervisors or City Council.
7. Go to your union meeting and get this resolution passed.

8. Wear a black armband.
9. Get together with some friends and buy a spot announcement on the radio indicating your opposition to the war.
10. Send a letter to all the magazines and newspapers to which you subscribe.
11. Call in to a radio talk show.
12. Talk to your neighbors and encourage them to do some of these activities.
13. Think up your own ideas and pass them on.

PLATE 61

YOU ARE ALREADY INVOLVED.

The myth of the "silent majority" is dead. We are all involved. It is no longer possible to avoid our responsibilities and to seek refuge in silence and apathy. Name calling, blind patriotism, and simplistic political cliches cannot negate 40,000 American war dead and the destruction of Southeast Asia and its people; nor can they negate the toll which this war and its consequences have inflicted upon American society. No escape can be found in the abdication of political responsibility. Each of us must examine the situation and recognize his position.

In the past few weeks, students and faculty from the nation's universities have taken positive measures to end U.S. military involvement in S.E. Asia. In an unprecedented effort to educate ourselves and the general public to the issues of the war and the implications within our society, the campus community has demonstrated the need for active participation. Writing, speaking, and lobbying have prevailed across the country. Such legitimate and necessary dissent must be reinforced by public support.

Personal action in a country as complex as ours often seems futile. But personal commitment is crucial for our society to face its problems and overcome them. Our form of government is based upon our legislators' representing our convictions. We must make these convictions known to them. Let us move together to bring to the attention of our fellow men their obligation to act and to support those who have made a commitment to ending the war. We must each recognize our personal responsibility to act, and move accordingly. We are already involved.

This statement has been sponsored by the students and faculties of University of California: at Berkeley, Davis, Irvine, Los Angeles, Riverside, Santa Barbara, Santa Cruz, San Diego, San Francisco; University of the Pacific; Claremont Mens College; Pitzer College; Pomona College; Stanford University; University of Southern California; San Jose State College; San Francisco State College; San Diego State College; San Fernando Valley State College; Hastings Law School; Boalt Law School; Mills College; Long Beach State College and their professional counterparts.

1.
TAKE PERSONAL ACTION:
Write; Campaign

Make a personal commitment to write 20 postcards to legislators expressing your opposition to the war—OR—pledge 20 hours of campaign time to a peace candidate of your choice.

2.
SUPPORT STATE LEGISLATION:
Vasconcellos Bill

This bill in Sacramento protects California residents from fighting in wars that have not received Congress' explicit approval and are thus unconstitutional. Write to Speaker of the Assembly Robert Monagan, State Capitol, Sacramento, and your local assemblyman.

3.
SUPPORT FEDERAL LEGISLATION:
McGovern-Hatfield Amendment

This amendment exercises Congress' power to control funds calling for a stoppage of funds for Cambodia 30 days after the passage of the amendment, stoppage of funds for military operations in S.E. Asia after June 30, 1971.

4.
CONTRIBUTE FUNDS:

Help the universities continue their peace efforts.

CONSTRUCTIVE ALTERNATIVES, R. Remen, Chmn.
1124 F Street, Apt. 21
Davis, California 95616

[ ] I pledge to write 20 postcards to legislators expressing my opposition to the war.
[ ] I pledge to work 20 hours in the next congressional campaign for a candidate who is against the war.

Name _____
Address _____
City, State _____

HON. CARL BRITSCHGI
State Capitol
Sacramento, Calif.

I endorse & urge the passage of the Vasconcellos bill, 1674.

Name _____
Address _____
City, State _____

SENATOR ALAN CRANSTON
U.S. Senate
Washington, D.C.

I endorse & urge the passage of the McGovern-Hatfield amendment.

Name _____
Address _____
City, State _____

CONSTRUCTIVE ALTERNATIVES, R. Remen, Chmn.
1124 F Street, Apt. 21
Davis, California 95616

I have enclosed $ _____
in [ ] Cash
[ ] Money Order
[ ] Check
To further the peace efforts to such as this ad.

Name _____
Address _____
City, State _____

PLATE 62

AMERICA SAYS:★

ACTIONS
SPEAK
LOUDER
THAN
WORDS

For the last nine years and three presidents America has been hearing that troops were being brought home from Southeast Asia as quickly as possible, yet today there are still more American Soldiers in Southeast Asia than ever before. How can we continue to believe in Nixon's desire to end the war when his every action denies this? Troops come and go; there are games of escalation and de-escalation, and the war keeps growing.

Likewise, most Americans say they are against the war, yet continue to do "business as usual." The actions of American students speak louder than Nixon's words. Universities everywhere are closing down and working against the war, and will do so until the last soldier is home. If Americans are really eager to end the war let us take direct action.

Some suggestions are provided here; let each of us act against the war in our own way, but let us, at least, ACT.

PROPOSALS:

1. Send "public service telegrams" indicating your opposition to the war to these officials elected by the people of San Francisco: **President Nixon** (The White House, Washington, D.C. 20500) **Senator Alan Cranston** or **Senator George Murphy** (New Senate Office Building, Washington, D.C. 20510), **Representative William Mailliard** (Rayburn House Office Building, Washington, D.C. 20515), and **Representative Phillip Burton** (Cannon House Office Building, Washington, D.C. 20515).

2. Start an economic boycott by restricting your purchases to necessary food and minimal living expenditures.

3. Telegrams in support of the **Vasconcellas bill** to put The California Assembly on record against the use of California citizens in the illegal and un-declared war in Southeast Asia. Send these to **Assemblymen Willie Brown, John Burton, John Foran** and **Leo McCarthy** at The State Capitol Building, Sacramento, California 95814.

4. Telegrams to **Assemblyman John Burton** in support of the introduction in the California Assembly of a motion to censure President Nixon.

5. If you have any Savings Bonds, sell them. If you are on the Payroll Savings Plan, withdraw from it. Besides being a poor investment, these bonds underwrite the war.

6. Do not pay your telephone tax. It was put on specifically to help pay for the war in Vietnam. Your phone will not be cut off. For further information on this tactic, call the War Resisters League at 626-6976.

7. Get your church to take a stand against the expansion of the war and communicate this stand to the press and to Washington.

8. Introduce resolutions into EVERY ORGANIZATION TO WHICH YOU BELONG. Get them to send a representative to Washington to lobby with others who are coming in from all over the country. Get your group to express this stand to the Board of Supervisors.

9. Go to your union meeting and get a resolution passed.

10. Wear a black arm-band.

11. Send a letter to the editor of the Chronicle or Examiner and any other paper to which you subscribe. Write to Time, Newsweek, Look, Life, etc.

12. Call in to radio talk shows.

13. Talk to your neighbors and encourage them to do some of these activities. Organize a block peace committee.

14. If you are a student join the student strike. If you are a parent, support your children by ensuring that their constitutional rights are protected and by taking some form of action against school or police harassment when it occurs.

15. Think up your own ideas and implement them.

Printed By Pacific Rotaprinting Co.

PLATE 63

PLATE 64

PLATE 65

PLATE 66

NOTES

1. The Penn State University Special Collections also house a set of photographs, taken by the author, of a "Gentle Thursday" celebration at Penn State, which shows another face of student style and sentiment during the Vietnam War; the Gentle Thursday photographs are online as well. Also available at Special Collections is a copy of a documentary film by P. J. O'Connell, *The Year Behind . . . and the Year Ahead*, documenting a sit-in at Old Main on the Penn State campus. Yet another Penn State University student demonstration, this one from 1972, is described in Thomas W. Benson, "Rhetoric as a Way of Being," in *American Rhetoric: Context and Criticism*, ed. Benson (Carbondale: Southern Illinois University Press, 1989), 293–322.

2. Jeffrey T. Schnapp, *Revolutionary Tides: The Art of the Political Poster, 1914–1989* (Milan: Skira, in association with the Iris and B. Gerald Cantor Center for Visual Arts at Stanford University, 2005), 20.

3. Margaret Timmers, introduction to *The Power of the Poster*, ed. Margaret Timmers (London: V&A Publishing, 1998), 8.

4. Richard M. Nixon, "Address to the Nation on the Situation in Southeast Asia," April 30, 1970, online at the American Presidency Project, http://www.presidency.ucsb.edu/ws/?pid=2490.

5. American action in Cambodia had actually, but secretly, been going on since early 1969, soon after Nixon's inauguration, when he ordered a bombing campaign designed to disrupt North Vietnamese supply routes. The bombings were so secret that they were "concealed even from top Air Force leaders"; see Maurice Isserman and Michael Kazin, *America Divided: The Civil War of the 1960s*, 4th ed. (New York: Oxford University Press, 2012), 251. The bombings contributed to the destruction of Cambodia's neutral government and the rise of the Khmer Rouge. On Senate opposition to the war, see Gary Stone, *Elites for Peace: The Senate and the Vietnam War, 1964–1968* (Knoxville: University of Tennessee Press, 2007). After the United States withdrew from Vietnam, the press was sometimes blamed, in American political debates, for undermining the war effort; a refutation of that view is offered by military historian William M. Hammond in *Reporting Vietnam: Media and Military at War* (Lawrence: University Press of Kansas, 1998).

6. James Reston, "Washington: 'The Heart of the Trouble,'" *New York Times*, May 3, 1970, ProQuest, accessed February 21, 2008. The photograph of Nixon delivering the speech is White House Photo Office Roll-Frame number WHPO 3448–21A, on file with the Richard Nixon Presidential Library and Museum.

7. Isserman and Kazin claim that "several dozen" ROTC buildings were burned down; they also note that "on the overwhelming majority of campuses, however, the protests were peaceful" (*America Divided*, 255).

8. Jean de Onis, "Nixon Puts 'Bums' Label on Some College Radicals," *New York Times*, May 2, 1970. Nixon was asked about the "bums"

remark in his press conference of May 8, four days after the killings at Kent State University, and, referring again to student protesters, said that "bums is perhaps too kind a word to apply to that kind of person." President's News Conference, May 8, 1970. Nixon's Pentagon remarks were recorded by an NBC TV news reporter and were played on the evening news on May 1, 1970. The moment can be seen and heard on the Vanderbilt Television News Archive online—http://tvnews.vanderbilt.edu/. In addition to referring to student dissenters as "bums," Nixon invoked memories of Nazi Germany with his reference to "burning the books" and "storming around."

9. William A. Gordon, *The Fourth of May: Killings and Coverups at Kent State* (Buffalo, NY: Prometheus Books, 1990), 22–24.

10. James Rhodes, quoted in Peter Davies, *The Truth About Kent State: A Challenge to the American Conscience* (New York: Farrar, Straus and Giroux, 1973), 21–22.

11. Del Corso, quoted by Davies in *Truth About Kent State*, 22.

12. Richard Nixon, "Statement on the Deaths of Four Students at Kent State University, Kent, Ohio," May 4, 1970, online at the American Presidency Project, http://www.presidency.ucsb.edu/ws/?pid=2492. Stanley Karnow, who blames Nixon's "inflammatory rhetoric" for initiating the spiral of vicious rhetoric that led to Kent State, calls the news conference statement "wanton insensitivity." Stanley Karnow, *Vietnam: A History* (New York: Penguin, 1991), 626.

13. Homer Bigart, "War Foes Here Attacked by Construction Workers," *New York Times*, May 9, 1970. The New Left's relations with the labor movement were complicated. Organized labor was committed to Cold War liberalism, and largely supported the war. The drift of American workers from the New Deal descendants of the 1960s to Reagan Democrats in 1980 is described in Jefferson R. Cowie, *Stayin' Alive: The 1970s and the Last Days of the Working Class* (New York: New Press, 2010). See also Peter B. Levy, *The New Left and Labor in the 1960s* (Urbana: University of Illinois Press, 1994).

14. Penny Lewis, *Hardhats, Hippies, and Hawks: The Vietnam Antiwar Movement as*

Myth and Memory (Ithaca: Cornell University Press, 2013); Christian G. Appy, *Working-Class War: American Combat Soldiers and Vietnam* (Chapel Hill: University of North Carolina Press, 1993); Michael S. Foley, *Confronting the War Machine: Draft Resistance During the Vietnam War* (Chapel Hill: University of North Carolina Press, 2003); Tracey A. Quigley, "Unheard and Unheeded: The Rhetoric of Military Dissent in the Debate over Vietnam" (PhD diss., Pennsylvania State University, 2005).

15. Richard Nixon, "The President's News Conference," May 8, 1970, online at the American Presidency Project, http://www.presidency.ucsb.edu/ws/?pid=2496.

16. Karnow, *Vietnam*, 626.

17. Ibid., 626–27.

18. See Robert Cohen, *Freedom's Orator: Mario Savio and the Radical Legacy of the 1960s* (New York: Oxford University Press, 2009); Robert Cohen and Reginald E. Zelnick, eds., *The Free Speech Movement: Reflections on Berkeley in the 1960s* (Berkeley: University of California Press, 2002).

19. *Berkeley Barb*, May 23–29, 1969.

20. Kathryn Bigelow's photograph can be found in Alan Copeland and Nikki Arai, eds., *People's Park* (New York: Ballantine Books, 1969), 55. This book, which immediately brought national and international attention to the events at People's Park, is based on an exhibit at the Phoenix Art Gallery in Berkeley, September–October 1969, that, according to the editors, drew an audience of more than 20,000. The photograph is reproduced in Berkeley Art Center Association, *The Whole World's Watching: Peace and Social Justice Movements of the 1960s and 1970s* (Berkeley, CA: Berkeley Art Center Association, 2001), 115. The book is based on an exhibition of photographs at the Berkeley Art Center, September–December 2001.

21. Hersh told the story of My Lai in three articles in the *St. Louis Post-Dispatch*, starting with Seymour Hersh, "Lieutenant Accused of Murdering 109 Civilians," *St. Louis Post-Dispatch*, November 25, 1969. The story immediately became an international sensation. Hersh was awarded the Pulitzer Prize for the series. The first story is reprinted in *Reporting Vietnam: Part Two; American Journalism,*

1969–1975 (New York: Library of America, 1998), 13–27.

22. Lou Cannon, *Governor Reagan: His Rise to Power* (New York: PublicAffairs, 2003), 295. Reagan had by this time caused enormous turmoil in California higher education. On February 22, 1968, San Francisco State College president John Summerskill resigned: "In his resignation statement, he charged the Reagan administration with 'political interference and financial starvation' of the State college system. 'I do not think we will see peace on our campus until we see peace in our cities, peace in Vietnam,' he said." William H. Orrick Jr., *Shut It Down! A College in Crisis: San Francisco State College, October 1968–April 1969* (Washington, DC: Government Printing Office, 1969), 27. On Ronald Reagan's "war on students," see Seth Rosenfeld, *Subversives: The FBI's War on Student Radicals, and Reagan's Rise to Power* (New York: Farrar, Straus and Giroux, 2012).

23. "Berkeley Tribe," *Wikipedia*, accessed March 25, 2012. In early March 1970, the *Tribe* editorialized that it was time to "pick up the gun."

24. In the interest of full disclosure, I should note that I suggested the language and the strategy of "On Strike—Keep It Open" to the student leaders in the early days of the strike, and both the phrase and the strategy seem to have stuck. NBC broadcast a special report on May 10, 1970—"Our House Divided." One discussant was Don Siegel, a Berkeley law student and former student government president, who explained that at Berkeley "we're going to strike to open it up." Siegel and I were both graduates of Hamilton College in Clinton, New York (as was Robert Moses, who led the Mississippi Freedom Summer); I mentioned this connection to Siegel when we talked in the student union in May 1970 and suggested the "On Strike—Keep It Open" idea. Siegel graduated from Hamilton some years after I did, and I had not known him before introducing myself to him in 1970. A number of the posters in the UC Archive collection of May 1970 posters advertise events held by various disciplines and departments investigating how their field could contribute to the moment, strong evidence that the "Keep It Open" idea spread through the campus.

25. This is a translation of an account, first published in French in a small book about the Atelier Populaire published in Paris: *Atelier Populaire: Présenté par lui-même; 87 affiches de mai–juin 1968* (Paris: Usines Universités Union, 1968). A translation of this book was published the next year as *Posters from the Revolution, Paris, May, 1968* (London: Dobson; Indianapolis: Bobbs-Merrill, 1969).

26. The Library of Congress site for the de Gaulle–Hitler poster is at http://www.loc.gov/pictures/item/99471822/. The de Gaulle poster is not shown in the collections of Atelier Populaire posters edited by Mark Rohan or Johan Kugelberg. It does appear in Serge Hambourg, *Protest in Paris 1968: Photographs by Serge Hambourg* (Hanover, NH: Hood Museum of Art, Dartmouth College, 2006), 76, where it is shown affixed to a wall.

27. "Hinter der Maske," unknown artist, poster, lithograph on paper, Collection of the Imperial War Museum, London, Art.IWM PST 5667.

28. Five years later, Jean-Paul Sartre published the essay "Elections: A Trap for Fools," in which, referring to the elections of 1968, won by de Gaulle, he argued that "each man . . . will choose his masters for the next four years without seeing that this so-called right to vote is simply the refusal to allow him to unite with others in resolving the true problems by *praxis*." Jean-Paul Sartre, "Elections: A Trap for Fools," in *Life / Situations*, trans. Paul Auster and Lydia Davis (New York: Pantheon, 1977), 204.

29. One probably very minor thread among the myriad possible connections is illustrated by the recollections of Franklin Rosemont. A self-identified anarchist from Chicago, Rosemont, who was editor of the obscure 1960s *Rebel Worker*, writes of meeting Guy Debord in Paris in the winter of 1965–66 and of bringing Situationist International materials back with him to Chicago, where they were circulated among his IWW, surrealist, and anarchist friends and sold from the related bookstore, Solidarity: "From May '66 through the end of '68, the Rebel Worker group did more to promote the Situationist International than any group in the U.S." Rosemont and Debord apparently came to see

that they had very different views, but these and other ideas and impulses were in circulation. Franklin Rosemont, "To Be Revolutionary in Everything: The Rebel Worker Story, 1964–68," in Franklin Rosemont and Charles Radcliffe, eds., *Dancin' in the Streets! Anarchists, IWWs, Surrealists, Situationists, and Provos in the 1960s as Recorded in the Pages of "The Rebel Worker" and "Heatwave"* (Chicago: Charles H. Kerr, 2005), 61. See also Penelope Rosemont, "Berkeley Was Only the Beginning," apparently from the July 1965 *Rebel Worker*, in Rosemont and Radcliffe, *Dancin' in the Streets*, 154–56; Rosemont quotes with approval a *New York Times* story alleging that the Berkeley student rebels of the time were as much anarchist or IWW as they were Marxist (155).

30. Guy Debord, *Society of the Spectacle* (Detroit: Black and Red, 1983), sec. 24.

31. The bibliography lists several histories of the 1960s, the New Left, and SDS. See especially Todd Gitlin, *The Sixties: Years of Hope, Days of Rage* (New York: Bantam Books, 1987), and *The Whole World Is Watching: Mass Media in the Making and Unmaking of the New Left* (Berkeley: University of California Press, 1980); Tom Hayden, *Reunion: A Memoir* (New York: Random House, 1988); David Burner, *Making Peace with the 60s* (Princeton: Princeton University Press, 1996); Tom Hayden, *The Port Huron Statement: The Visionary Call of the 1960s Revolution* (New York: Thunder's Mouth Press, 2005).

32. Some posters circulating in Berkeley in 1970 may have been more militant than those in the Penn State collection. A photograph from the time shows a college-aged woman sitting on the steps of Sproul Hall with a poster captioned "Victory to the N.L.F." Nacio Jan Brown, "Anti-Vietnam War Rally: Sproul Steps, University of California Berkeley, Late 1960s," in *The Whole World's Watching*, 36. A poster that I have seen only in the UC Archives reads, "Why the School is Closed Today & you white Amerikan students right on! With yr struggle agains the Kent murders. Only 7 weeks in Cambodia the wicked messenger says. The fool, the Oriental People's will be there for 10 thousand years after Amerika falls. you racists, what about North Carolina where

they sprayed the dormitories with machine gun fire? KIDNAP DIPLOMATS: RANSOM BOBBY.— berkeley May 1970." UC Archives, Ff308h. R311p, Box 2. The poster seems to self-identify as coming from outside the campus.

33. Philippe Vermés quoted in William Bostwick, "Rock Versus Paper," *Print* 66, no. 1 (February 2012): 56.

34. Atelier Populaire, *Posters from the Revolution*, 3.

35. John Barnicoat, "Poster," in *Grove Art Online / Oxford Art Online*, accessed April 10, 2012, http://www.oxfordartonline.com/subscriber/article/grove/art/T068980.

36. Michael Seidman, *The Imaginary Revolution: Parisian Students and Workers in 1968* (New York: Berghahn Books, 2003), 130.

37. Ibid., 12.

38. Marc Rohan, *Paris '68: Graffiti, Posters, Newspapers, and Poems of the Events of May 1968* (London: Impact Books, 1988), 36.

39. "Oral History Interview with Rupert Garcia, 7 September 1995–24 June 1996" (Oakland, California), Archives of American Art, Smithsonian Institution. This passage is also quoted in Lincoln Cushing, *All of Us or None: Social Justice Posters of the San Francisco Bay Area* (Berkeley, CA: Heyday, 2012), 19–22.

40. See, for example, "Viet Nam Day May 21 & 22," a poster from 1965, preserved as part of the docspopuli online collection of Lincoln Cushing—http://www.docspopuli.org/BHScat/detail.np/detail-01.html. The poster was exhibited April–September 2009 at the Berkeley Historical Center. The online exhibit notes, "Curated by archivist and poster scholar Lincoln Cushing, this exhibition is drawn from a unique private Berkeley collection of over 25,000 political posters assembled by Free Speech Movement activist Michael Rossman," http://www.docspopuli.org/articles/BHS2009.html. Cushing is the author of *Revolucion! Cuban Poster Art* (San Francisco: Chronicle Books, 2003); *Agitate! Educate! Organize! American Labor Posters* (Ithaca, NY: ILR Press, 2009); with Ann Tompkins, *Chinese Posters: Art from the Great Proletarian Cultural Revolution* (San Francisco: Chronicle Books, 2007); and *All of Us or None*. See also Michael Rossman, "The Evolution of the Social Serigraphy Movement

in the San Francisco Bay Area, 1966–1986," http://mrossman.org/posters/socialseri graphy/socialserigraphy.html.

41. Walter Medeiros, "Inside Drawn Out," in Gayle Lemke and Jacaeber Kastor, *The Art of the Fillmore, 1966–1971* (New York: Thunder's Mouth Press, 1997), 100.

42. Bill Graham, quoted in Lemke and Kastor, *Art of the Fillmore*, 15.

43. Edward Marc Treib, "California Street Scene: Getting the Message in Berkeley," *Print* 28 (1974): 67–68.

44. Alton Kelley, quoted in Lemke and Kastor, *Art of the Fillmore*, 100.

45. Kevin M. Moist, "A Grounded Situational Assessment of Meanings Emerging from the Consideration of Psychedelic Rock Concert Posters as a Form of Subcultural Visionary Rhetoric" (PhD diss., University of Iowa, 2000), 140.

46. Matthieu Poirer, "Hyper-optical and Kinetic Stimulation, 'Happenings,' and Films in France," in *Summer of Love: Psychedelic Art, Social Crisis, and Counterculture in the 1960s*, ed. Christoph Grunenberg and Jonathan Harris (Liverpool: Liverpool University Press, 2005), 281–83, 297.

47. Andrew Wilson, "Spontaneous Underground: An Introduction to London Psychedelic Scenes, 1965–1968," in Grunenberg and Harris, *Summer of Love*, 91. It is worth noting that because of the volatility of "Marxism" in any discussion of American rhetoric, the "even Marxian" analysis seemingly endorsed by Wilson was present in some genealogies of the New Left in the United States; the movement rhetoric as a whole, however, was typically not explicitly Marxist in its appeals—and the Berkeley posters appear to be much more a part of the non-Marxist liberal peace movement.

48. Walter Medeiros, "Mapping San Francisco, 1965–1967: Roots and Florescence of the San Francisco Counterculture," in Grunenberg and Harris, *Summer of Love*, 303–48.

49. James T. Patterson, *The Eve of Destruction: How 1965 Transformed America* (New York: Basic Books, 2012), xiii.

50. See, for example, Jules Witcover, *The Year the Dream Died: Revisiting 1968 in America* (New York: Warner Books, 1997); Michael T.

Kaufman, *1968* (New York: Roaring Brook Press, 2009); Donald Myrus, ed., *Law and Disorder: The Chicago Convention and Its Aftermath* (Chicago: Donald Myrus and Burton Joseph, 1968).

51. See Ralph E. Shikes, *The Indignant Eye: The Artist as Social Critic in Prints and Drawings from the Fifteenth Century to Picasso* (Boston: Beacon Press, 1976); William M. Ivins Jr., *Prints and Visual Communication* (Cambridge, MA: Harvard University Press, 1953); Leslie Shepard, *The History of Street Literature: The Story of Broadside Ballads, Chapbooks, Proclamations, News-sheets, Election Bills, Tracts, Pamphlets, Cocks, Catchpennies, and Other Ephemera* (Detroit: Singing Tree Press, 1973). Georgia B. Bumgardner, noting that the first broadside was printed by Gutenberg in 1454, reports that "the first American broadside was 'The Oath of a Free Man,' printed by Stephen Daye in Cambridge in 1679." Georgia B. Bumgardner, *American Broadsides* (Barre, MA: Imprint Society, 1971), n.p. At about the time the Berkeley posters were produced, a UC Berkeley folklorist was conducting a study of public-bathroom graffiti in Berkeley; see Alan Dundes, "Here I Sit—A Study of American Latrinalia," in Dundes, *Analytic Essays in Folklore* (The Hague: Mouton, 1975), 177–91.

52. Roger G. Kennedy and David Larkin, *When Art Worked: The New Deal, Art, and Democracy* (New York: Rizzoli, 2009), 21. See also Ann Prentice Wagner, *1934: A New Deal for Artists* (Washington, DC: Smithsonian American Art Museum, 2009); Bruce I. Bustard, *A New Deal for the Arts* (Washington, DC, and Seattle, WA: National Archives and Records Administration in association with the University of Washington Press, 1997); Allen Cohen and Ronald L. Filippelli, *Times of Sorrow and Hope: Documenting Everyday Life in Pennsylvania During the Depression and World War II* (University Park: Pennsylvania State University Press, 2003); Cara A. Finnegan, *Picturing Poverty: Print Culture and FSA Photographs* (Washington, DC: Smithsonian Institution Scholarly Press, 2003).

53. Kennedy and Larkin, *When Art Worked*, 25.

54. Christopher DeNoon, *Posters of the WPA* (Los Angeles: Wheatley Press, 1987), 13,

26–29, 32. In the 1960s, just across the Bay from Berkeley, in San Rafael, California, Mary Perry Stone was creating murals and paintings on progressive social themes, including a long series protesting the Vietnam War. I know of no evidence that the Berkeley poster artists knew of the work by Stone, who had been in New York as a sculptor on the Federal Arts Project. But hers is perhaps one of many examples of the links between the generation of progressive WPA artists and the public of 1970 that could have seen her work and the Berkeley posters within a few miles of each other. This account of Mary Perry Stone is based on recollections by her daughter, Ramie Strong, in letters to the author on May 22, 2012, and May 24, 2012. Ramie Strong recalls that her mother's WPA sculptures were lost when they were discarded from the warehouse in New York where they had been stored. Some of Mary Perry Stone's work may be seen at http://maryperrystone.com. Richard Nixon became a member of the Un-American Activities Committee after his election to Congress in 1946; he first came to fame when Whittaker Chambers testified before the committee that Alger Hiss had become, like Chambers, a Communist agent, leading to a sensational trial and the conviction of Hiss on a perjury charge. Nixon's very public role in the affair vaulted him to the Senate in 1950 and the vice presidency in 1952.

55. The Library of Congress collection may be consulted at http://www.loc.gov/pictures/collection/wpapos/about.html. The Living Archive is online at http://postersforthepeople.com/.

56. Anthony Velonis, *Silk Screen Technique* (New York: Creative Crafts Press, 1939), 1–2.

57. Franklin Delano Roosevelt, "Rear Platform Remarks at Hayfield, Minnesota," October 9, 1936, online at the American Presidency Project, Santa Barbara, CA, http://www.presidency.ucsb.edu/ws/?pid=15155.

58. DeNoon, *Posters of the WPA*, 31.

59. Pearl James, "Introduction: Reading World War I Posters," in *Picture This: World War I Posters and Visual Culture*, ed. James (Lincoln: University of Nebraska Press, 2009), 2.

60. William L. Bird Jr. and Harry R. Rubenstein, *Design for Victory: World War II Posters on the American Home Front* (New York: Princeton Architectural Press, 1998), 1. For a recent rhetorical analysis of World War II posters, see Susan B. Barnes, "Don't Let Him Down! WWII Propaganda Posters," in *Visual Impact: The Power of Visual Persuasion*, ed. Barnes (Cresskill, NJ: Hampton Press, 2009), 95–116.

61. Bird and Rubenstein, *Design for Victory*, 1–2.

62. Ibid., 31.

63. Ibid., 98. Among the most enduring World War II posters in American collective memory are "We Can Do It!"—the Rosie the Riveter poster—and the Four Freedoms series based on paintings by Norman Rockwell. On the rhetoric of these posters, see Lester C. Olson, "Portraits in Praise of a People: A Rhetorical Analysis of Norman Rockwell's Icons in Franklin D. Roosevelt's 'Four Freedoms' Campaign," *Quarterly Journal of Speech* 69, no. 1 (February 1983): 15–24, and James J. Kimble and Lester C. Olson, "Visual Rhetoric Representing Rosie the Riveter: Myth and Misconception in J. Howard Miller's 'We Can Do It!' Poster," *Rhetoric and Public Affairs* 9, no. 4 (Winter 2006): 533–69.

64. On the reemergence of politics in modern art in the 1960s, see Paul Wood, Francis Frascina, Jonathan Harris, and Charles Harrison, *Modernism in Dispute: Art Since the Forties* (New Haven: Yale University Press, 1993). On the other hand, a standard college survey of art history, first published in 1962, devotes but one paragraph to the poster as part of a discussion of twentieth-century photography (about which the author raises the question "Is it art?"). H. W. Janson, *History of Art*, 3rd ed. (New York: Harry N. Abrams; Englewood Cliffs, NJ: Prentice-Hall, 1986), 778. The 572-page first edition of *History of Art* has no index entry for posters: H. W. Janson, *History of Art* (New York: Harry N. Abrams, 1962). Although he also does not devote much attention to posters, E. H. Gombrich notes the interplay of fine and commercial art in his discussion of modern and experimental art of the twentieth century: "Many who have no use for what they call 'this ultra-modern stuff' would be surprised to learn how much of it has entered their lives already, and has helped to mould their taste and their preferences. Forms

and colour schemes which were developed by ultra-modern rebels in painting have become the common stock-in-trade of commercial art; and when we meet them on posters, magazine covers or fabrics, they look quite normal to us." E. H. Gombrich, *The Story of Art*, 12th ed. (London: Phaidon Press, 1972), 445.

65. David Kunzle, *American Posters of Protest, 1966–70: Art as a Political Weapon* (New York: New School Art Center, 1971), 6. See also Kunzle, *L'Era di Johnson: Manifesti della gioventù studentesca e pacifista americana* (Milan: La Pietra, 1968); Kunzle, *Posters of Protest: The Posters of Political Satire in the U.S., 1966–1970* (Santa Barbara: University of California Press, 1971); Maurice Berger, *Representing Vietnam, 1965–1973: The Antiwar Movement in America* (New York: The Bertha and Karl Leubsdorf Art Gallery, 1988); Nina Castelli Sundell, Cleveland Center for Contemporary Art, and Lehman College Art Gallery, *The Turning Point: Art and Politics in 1968* (Cleveland, OH: Cleveland Center for Contemporary Art, 1988); Lucy R. Lippard, *A Different War: Vietnam in Art* (Seattle, WA: Whatcom Museum of History and Art and Real Comet Press, 1990); and Susan Martin, ed., *Decade of Protest: Political Posters from the United States, Viet Nam, Cuba, 1965–1975* (Santa Monica, CA: Smart Art Press, 1996). Lippard and Sundell offer especially important early reflections on Americans artists who turned to protest themes. Most recently, a comprehensive study of American artists taking up political themes in the period is Matthew Israel, *Kill for Peace: American Artists Against the Vietnam War* (Austin: University of Texas Press, 2013), which was published after the present study was going to press. Israel includes one of the Berkeley posters in his study—Jay Belloli's "Amerika Is Devouring Its Children"—on p. 54.

66. I collected posters on campus and retained them until about 2008, when I donated them to the Pennsylvania State University Libraries, Special Collections, Historical and Labor Archives.

67. Cushing, *All of Us or None*, 23.

68. Ibid., 24. In a note about this book, Tom Hayden recalled that "during the Indochina Peace Campaign (1969–73), my students at Immaculate Heart College under the supervision of Sr. Corita Kent produced hundreds of silk-screens depicting the war and Vietnamese culture, which were packaged so that they could be sent and set up on any stage anywhere. There were hundreds of showings. The original collection is in my archives in Ann Arbor" (Tom Hayden, email correspondence with Kendra Boileau, July 21, 2014). Hayden adds that "the posters from Cuba were a driving creative force everywhere in the late '60s," and that "the Panther posters by Emory . . . came out weekly, distributed with 100,000 copies of the Panther paper for a time."

69. Peter Selz, *Art of Engagement: Visual Politics in California and Beyond* (Berkeley: University of California Press, 2005), 261n14.

70. Francis Frascina, *Art, Politics, and Dissent: Aspects of the Art Left in Sixties America* (Manchester: Manchester University Press, 1999), 184. On My Lai and its cultural memories, see Kendrick Oliver, *The My Lai Massacre in American History and Memory* (Manchester: Manchester University Press, 2006). Nick Turse, *Kill Anything that Moves: The Real American War in Vietnam* (New York: Henry Holt, 2013), argues that My Lai has wrongly come to be remembered as an exceptional act of wanton violence; instead, says Turse, "murder, torture, rape, abuse, forced displacement, home burnings, specious arrests, imprisonment without due process" were "virtually a daily fact of life throughout the years of the American presence in Vietnam. . . . They were the inevitable outcome of deliberate policies, dictated at the highest levels of the military" (6). The photograph used in the "And Babies" poster was reprinted in the *Berkeley Barb*, March 20–26, 1970.

71. Berkeley Poster Collection, University of British Columbia Rare Books and Special Collections, Berkeley Folder 38, poster 187.

72. See http://news.bbc.co.uk/2/shared/spl/hi/picture_gallery/05/in_pictures_the_vietnam_war_/html/11.stm, accessed August 1, 2012.

73. The photograph, identified as UPI/Bettman Archive, appears in Marilyn B. Young, *The Vietnam Wars, 1945–1990* (New York: HarperCollins, 1991), between pp. 242 and 243.

74. "War Is Unhealthy for America" is apparently a variation on a popular poster from

1967 by Lorraine Art Schneider, "War Is Not Healthy for Children and Other Living Things," part of the campaign of a group called Another Mother for Peace.

75. On the iconic photograph of the Kent State shootings, see Robert Hariman and John Louis Lucaites, *No Caption Needed: Iconic Photographs, Public Culture, and Liberal Democracy* (Chicago: University of Chicago Press, 2007).

76. In his memoirs, Ulysses S. Grant observed of opposition to the Mexican War that "once initiated there were but few public men who would have the courage to oppose it. Experience proves that the man who obstructs a war in which his nation is engaged, no matter whether right or wrong, occupies no enviable place in life or history. Better for him to advocate 'war, pestilence, and famine,' than to act as obstructionist to a war already begun." Ulysses S. Grant, *Memoirs and Selected Letters* (New York: Library of America, 1990), 50.

77. Adam Folk, "Residents Recall 1970 Riot that Rocked Augusta," *Augusta Chronicle*, May 10, 2010. The Augusta uprising was described by Georgia governor Lester Maddox, an infamous racist who owed his election to an incident in which he had barred African Americans from his restaurant by threatening them with an ax handle, as proof of outside Communist influence.

78. The crowd has a varied rhetorical history. See especially *Crowds*, ed. Jeffrey T. Schnapp and Matthew Tiews (Stanford: Stanford University Press, 2006).

79. On the rhetoric of the Norman Rockwell Four Freedoms series, see Olson, "Portraits in Praise of a People," 15–24.

80. Posters are specifically described as a mode of nonviolent action in Gene Sharp, *The Politics of Nonviolent Action* (Boston: Porter Sargent, 1973); see 2:125–27. Sharp originally wrote the work as his Oxford University doctoral dissertation, which was completed in 1968.

81. One or two of the posters in the Berkeley collection at the University of California Archives do appear to advocate violence directly.

82. Garth S. Jowett and Victoria O'Donnell, *Propaganda and Persuasion*, 4th ed. (Thousand Oaks, CA: Sage, 2006), 7, 31–32.

83. See, for example, Stephen Howard Browne, "Rhetorical Criticism and the Challenges of Bilateral Argument," *Philosophy and Rhetoric* 40 (2007): 108–18; Henry W. Johnstone Jr., "The Philosophical Basis of Rhetoric," *Philosophy and Rhetoric* 40, no. 1 (2007): 15–26.

84. The *Peanuts* comic strip (1950–2000) would have been well known to the artists and viewers of the posters in 1970. The cover illustration in Charles M. Schulz, *Security Is a Thumb and a Blanket* (San Francisco: Determined Productions, 1963), is the model for the 1970 Nixon poster "Security Is a Silent Majority." Each of the panels in *Security Is a Thumb* introduces a variation on "security is . . . ," with a facing-page illustration. The *Peanuts* comic appeared daily and on Sunday in many American newspapers. Linus and his blanket were a recurring theme. As early as July 6, 1951, the strip mentions the importance of a "feeling of security." On July 14, 1952, Lucy tells Charlie that she has a baby brother at home; Linus appears for the first time on September 19, 1952, and we learn his name on September 22, 1952. On June 1, 1954, Linus first uses a security blanket. On October 17, 1954, Lucy tells Charlie Brown that the blanket "gives him security and happiness." Charlie Brown gets his own blanket and tells Lucy it is a "'security and happiness' blanket" on October 24, 1954. Charles M. Schulz, *The Complete Peanuts, 1950 to 1952* (Seattle, WA: Fantagraphics Books, 2004), 80, 215, 243, 245; Schulz, *The Complete Peanuts, 1953 to 1954* (Seattle, WA: Fantagraphics Books, 2004), 222, 281, 284. The security blanket did not appear in the comic in 1969 or 1970, but it appears at least sixteen times in the years 1967–68, by which time it had been long established. See Charles M. Schulz, *The Complete Peanuts, 1967 to 1968* (Seattle, WA: Fantagraphics Books, 2008); and Schulz, *The Complete Peanuts, 1969 to 1970* (Seattle, WA: Fantagraphics Books, 2008). A forty-six-minute animated video, *Happiness Is a Warm Blanket, Charlie Brown*, was released in 2011, as was a companion graphic novel, *Happiness Is a Warm Blanket, Charlie Brown!* (Los Angeles, CA: Kaboom!, 2011). The "happiness is" motif was generative in popular culture. *Happiness Is . . . a Warm Puppy*, the first book by Charles Schulz, was published in 1962 and was often reissued, with variations. In the first cartoon in

the book, Linus sits sucking his thumb and holding his blanket to his left ear; the facing-page caption reads, "Happiness is a thumb and a blanket." It is the same cartoon that was used, with a different caption, in *Security Is a Thumb and a Blanket* the next year. The Beatles song "Happiness Is a Warm Gun," by John Lennon and Paul McCartney, was released as part of *The Beatles* (*The White Album*) in November 1968. See *The Beatles Lyrics* (Milwaukee WI: Hal Leonard, 1996).

Other posters also draw on popular art and memory, such as plate 28, "Let There Be Peace and Let It Begin with Me," which may allude to a 1955 song by Jill Jackson Miller and Sy Miller, "Let There Be Peace on Earth." A poster in the University of California Archives, Bancroft Library, Berkeley, depicts the *Peanuts* beagle Snoopy sitting on his doghouse, in World War I aviator helmet and goggles, silk scarf flying, a bird sitting on his nose. Snoopy is raising one paw in the familiar "curse you, Red Baron" gesture; a peace symbol is painted on the roof of the doghouse. The text at the bottom of the poster reads, "Nix on Agnew"; the "X" in "Nix" is replaced with a swastika (UC Archives, "Reconstitution of the Campus: Anti-war Posters Created and Distributed on the University of California, Berkeley Campus," May 1970, ff308h.R311p, Box 3). A version of the cartoon used in the "Security Is a Silent Majority" poster appeared, without caption and somewhat truncated, in the *Berkeley Barb*, March 20–26, 1970. The *Barb* version differs in small respects from the drawing in the poster; for example, in the poster, Nixon's T-shirt has broad alternating dark and white horizontal stripes, whereas in the *Barb* cartoon the stripes are indicated by narrow lines.

85. Richard Nixon, "Address to the Nation on the War in Vietnam," November 3, 1969, online at the American Presidency Project, http://www.presidency.ucsb.edu/ws/?pid =2303.

86. On "security" as the central theme of the New Deal, see David M. Kennedy, *Freedom from Fear: The American People in Depression and War, 1929–1945* (New York: Oxford University Press, 1999), 245: "Security was the touchstone, the single word that summed up more of what Roosevelt aimed at than any

other." On the cultural shifts of the 1950s and 1960s, see Gitlin, *The Sixties*.

87. Robert P. Newman, "Under the Veneer: Nixon's Vietnam Speech of November 3, 1969," *Quarterly Journal of Speech* 56, no. 2 (1970): 174, 176.

88. Ibid., 178.

89. Disciplinary effects were most evident in the arts, humanities, and social sciences, although in given cases academics in the sciences either participated in the war debates or turned their professional attention to related issues.

90. On implicit communication theory, see Thomas W. Benson, "Implicit Communication Theory in Campaign Coverage," in *Television Coverage of the 1980 Presidential Campaign*, ed. William C. Adams (Norwood, NJ: Ablex Publishing, 1983), 103–16.

91. Hermann G. Stelzner, "The Quest Story and Nixon's November 3, 1969 Address," *Quarterly Journal of Speech* 57, no. 2 (1971): 172.

92. Karlyn Kohrs Campbell, "An Exercise in the Rhetoric of Mythic America," in *Critiques of Contemporary Rhetoric* (Belmont, CA: Wadsworth, 1972), 50, 56.

93. The term "neo-Aristotelian" as applied to rhetorical criticism became a leading subject of discussion among rhetorical critics with the publication of Edwin R. Black, *Rhetorical Criticism: A Study in Method* (New York: Macmillan, 1965). Black used the term "neo-Aristotelian" to designate what he identified as a narrow, mechanical, and exhausted model for rhetorical criticism, voicing and giving focus to a widespread and building impatience with the reigning assumptions of the discipline. Both Black and Hill were doctoral students of Herbert A. Wichelns in the rhetoric program at Cornell University, where they were friends and classmates. I was in the doctoral program a few years behind, but overlapping, Black and Hill. Wichelns was the author of what had long been regarded as the founding text for rhetorical criticism, with its revival in America in the twentieth century—"The Literary Criticism of Oratory," in *Studies in Rhetoric and Public Speaking in Honor of James A. Winans*, ed. A. M. Drummond (New York: Century, 1925). See also Thomas W. Benson, "The Cornell School of Rhetoric: Idiom and

Institution," *Communication Quarterly* 51 (2003): 1–56; Benson, "Edwin Black: A Tribute," *Rhetoric and Public Affairs* 4 (2001): 535–39; and Benson, "Edwin Black's Cornell University," *Rhetoric and Public Affairs* 10 (2007): 481–88.

94. Forbes Hill, "Conventional Wisdom— Traditional Form—The President's Message of November 3, 1969," *Quarterly Journal of Speech* 58, no. 4 (December 1972): 374.

95. Jeffrey K. Tulis, *The Rhetorical Presidency* (Princeton: Princeton University Press, 1987), 128–29. Some rhetorical scholars have suggested that Tulis is adopting too narrow a view of rhetoric, and that, under a broader view, presidents have been rhetorical since the founding. See, for example, Martin J. Medhurst, ed., *Beyond the Rhetorical Presidency* (College Station: Texas A&M University Press, 1996).

96. Richard Nixon, who proclaimed that he would not be moved by student demonstrations, was apparently moved by Hollywood. He reportedly watched the film *Patton* several times in the spring of 1970 and found it deeply arousing, even going so far as to acquire a copy for his own use. Ronald H. Carpenter and Robert V. Seltzer report that the film had a "profound effect" on Nixon and suggest that "perhaps Richard Nixon himself was persuaded by *Patton* to take a hard line on the Viet Nam War and undertake the Cambodian Incursion. More likely, perhaps he sensed a widespread receptiveness on the part of the Silent Majority to a Pattonesque approach to the decision he had to make in April, 1970." Ronald H. Carpenter and Robert V. Seltzer, "Nixon, *Patton*, and a Silent Majority Sentiment About the Viet Nam War: The Cinematographic Bases of a Rhetorical Stance," *Central States Speech Journal* 25 (Summer 1974): 105, 110. *Patton* premiered in New York City on February 4, 1970, three months after the silent majority speech, and three months before the Cambodian incursion.

97. On quiescence, see Murray Edelman, *Politics as Symbolic Action: Mass Arousal and Quiescence* (New York: Academic Press, 1971).

98. After Pearl Harbor, and in some cases in the months leading up to it, when it appeared to most that US entry might be inevitable, isolationist dissent was sometimes depicted as disloyal, but the appeal to silence was almost always linked to the protection of military secrets. The silence theme also appeared in World War I posters: a British poster from about 1916 shows a woman with a golden helmet, her figure wrapped in the flag, gesturing with right index finger in front of her lips; printed on the poster are the words "SILENCE / DO NOT TALK. When you know that your unit is making preparations for an attack, don't talk about them to men in other units or to strangers, and keep your mouth shut, especially in public places. Do not be inquisitive about what other units are doing; if you hear or see anything, keep it to yourself. If you hear anyone else talking about operations, stop him at once. The success of the operations and the lives of your comrades depend upon your silence." Anonymous, "Silence," ca. 1916, in Walton Rawls, *Wake Up, America! World War I and the American Poster* (New York: Abbeville Press, 1988), 35. Jeffrey T. Schnapp observes in *Revolutionary Tides* that in political poster art,

> Ideally, the political crowd speaks in the single voice of virtue and truth, either as a chorus or as an individual entrusted with the task of representing the collectivity. In reality, it is a realm of differences and debate, animated by a mix of facts, opinions, impressions, gossip, public secrets, and private information that can become an object of scrutiny both by the state and by its enemies, particularly during times of social turmoil and military conflict. Exposed to the vast proliferation of information and technologies of eavesdropping and surveillance, the public receives a mixed message. Exercise your freedoms, discipline your mouth and ears. (66)

99. Silent majority" in *Oxford English Dictionary*, online, September 24, 2012. C. V. Wedgwood, *The King's Peace: 1637–1641* (New York: Macmillan, 1956), 256.

100. William Safire, "silent majority," in *Safire's New Political Dictionary: The Definitive Guide to the New Language of Politics* (New York: Random House, 1993), 707–9.

101. Ibid., 709. See also Safire's entry on "silent vote."

102. John F. Kennedy, *Profiles in Courage* (New York: HarperCollins, 1964), 253.

103. See Thomas W. Benson, "'To Lend a Hand': Gerald Ford, Watergate, and the White House Speechwriters," *Rhetoric and Public Affairs* 1 (1998): 201–25.

104. Spiro T. Agnew, "'The Responsibilities of Television,' Address before the Midwest Regional Republican Committee Meeting, Des Moines, November 13, 1969," in Agnew, *Frankly Speaking: A Collection of Extraordinary Speeches* (Washington, DC: Public Affairs Press, 1970), 62.

105. Rick Perlstein, *Nixonland: The Rise of a President and the Fracturing of America* (New York: Charles Scribner's Sons, 2008), 440.

106. The sentence "Don't just do something, stand there" is sometimes attributed to Peter Ustinov as corrective advice to method actors; the saying also appears in the tea party scene in the Disney animated film *Alice in Wonderland* (1951).

107. Spiro T. Agnew, "'Masochism Versus the Facts,' Address at Citizens' Testimonial Dinner, New Orleans, October 19, 1969," in Agnew, *Frankly Speaking*, 25.

108. Spiro T. Agnew, "'Impudence in the Streets,' Address at Pennsylvania Republican Dinner, Harrisburg, October 30, 1969," in Agnew, *Frankly Speaking*, 47–48.

109. See, for example, John Wesley Hanson Jr. and Lillian Woodward Gunckel, eds., *The Ideal Orator and Manual of Elocution, Containing a Practical Treatise on the Delsarte System of Physical Culture and Expression* (Springfield, IL: Home Education Publishing House, 1895).

110. Plate 11 is identified as having been created by Kamakazi Design Group and printed by Berkeley Graphics, a commercial printing firm. The poster contains a typographical error; I have silently corrected it in this book.

111. The poster contains a misspelling; I have silently corrected it in this book.

112. North Star, "Rise Up Angry!!! No More Lying Down," *Berkeley Barb*, May 8–14, 1970. The Eddie Adams photographs of General Nguyen Ngoc Loan executing a North Vietnam officer on the street are reproduced in *Eddie Adams: Vietnam*, ed. Alyssa Adams (New York: Umbrage, 2008), 142–51. The *Berkeley Barb* photograph may also be seen in Geoff Kaplan, ed., *Power to the People: The Graphic Design of the Radical Press and the Rise of the Counter-Culture, 1964–1974* (Chicago: University of Chicago Press, 2013), 213.

113. For a history of the "child at gunpoint" photograph, see Richard Raskin, *A Child at Gunpoint: A Case Study in the Life of a Photo* (Aarhus, Denmark: Aarhus University Press, 2004); see also Barbie Zelizer, *Remembering to Forget: Holocaust Memory Through the Camera's Eye* (Chicago: University of Chicago Press, 1998), and Hariman and Lucaites, *No Caption Needed*, 7. In a review of Raskin's book, Oren Baruch Stier raises an ethical and interpretive issue about uses of Holocaust images in later political contexts—an issue that lurks in several of the posters in the Berkeley collection. See Oren Baruch Stier, review of *A Child at Gunpoint*, by Richard Raskin, *Holocaust Genocide Studies* 20, no. 2 (Fall 2006): 309–11.

114. In full, it said: "This statement has been sponsored by the students and faculties of University of California: at Berkeley, Davis, Irvine, Los Angeles, Riverside, Santa Barbara, Santa Cruz, San Diego, San Francisco; University of the Pacific; Claremont Mens College; Pitzer College; Pomona College; Stanford University; University of Southern California; San Jose State College; San Francisco State College; San Diego State College; San Fernando Valley State College; Hastings Law School; Boalt Law School; Mills College; Long Beach State College and their professional counterparts."

115. On the rhetoric of photography, see Hariman and Lucaites, *No Caption Needed*; Finnegan, *Picturing Poverty*; Susan Sontag, *On Photography* (New York: Farrar, Straus and Giroux, 1977); and Zelizer, *Remembering to Forget*. Sontag writes, "The attempts by photographers to bolster up a depleted sense of reality contribute to the depletion. . . . Cameras are the antidote and the disease, a means of appropriating reality and a means of making it obsolete" (179).

116. Carlo Ginzburg, "'Your Country Needs You': A Case Study in Political Iconography," *History Workshop Journal*, no. 52 (Autumn 2001), 8. Ginzburg had apparently not seen the "Actions Speak Louder Than Words" poster, but he does discuss another anti–Vietnam War poster in which a bandaged Uncle Sam reaches out a supplicating hand with the words "I Want Out" (16), and he notes that the Kitchener poster had

itself been seen as suggesting something of George Orwell's Big Brother—a connection certainly emphasized by the Berkeley artists in their depictions of Nixon and Agnew. The "Uncle Sam Wants You" poster of 1917 inspired other protest posters: Kunzle's *L'Era di Johnson* includes "UNCLE SAM WANTS YOU!" with a figure of Uncle Sam in red, white, and blue pointing a revolver at the viewer (fig. 23, p. 23); "TURN OFF / TUNE OUT / DROP IN" (designed by John Thompson, printed in 1967 by Astro Posters, Berkeley, CA; fig. 24, p. 23), showing Lyndon Johnson as Uncle Sam recruiting the viewer to the psychedelic revolution; "JOIN," with a pudgy man in Uncle Sam costume, hand outstretched toward the viewer, with palm up, before the Capitol in Washington (fig. 25, p. 24; photo by Edmund Shea, American News Repeat Co., San Francisco); and "QUACK!" with Donald Duck, or perhaps his uncle Scrooge McDuck, as Uncle Sam pointing and glaring at the viewer (fig. 26, p. 24). A semiotic analysis of the "demand" presented by Kitchener's gaze and pointing finger appears in Gunther Kress and Theo van Leeuwen, *Reading Images: The Grammar of Visual Design*, 2nd ed. (London: Routledge, 2006), 117–18; this reading is consistent with a rhetorical approach, which would on the other hand be likely to suggest that every image asks something of the viewer, though not, as Kress and van Leeuwen acknowledge, in a form that is experienced as direct address. An analysis of the James Montgomery Flagg poster may also be found in W. J. T. Mitchell, *What Do Pictures Want? The Lives and Loves of Images* (Chicago: University of Chicago Press, 2005), 36–38: "You might think it a wonder that this poster had any power or effectiveness at all as a recruiting device, and indeed, it would be very difficult to know anything about the real power of the image. What one can describe, however, is its construction of desire in relation to fantasies of power and impotence. Perhaps the image's subtle candor about its bloodless sterility as well as its origins in commerce and caricature combine to make it seem so appropriate a symbol of the United States" (38).

117. Kenneth Burke tried to clarify some of the equivocations and ambiguities of "action" version "symbol" by attributing "action" to humans and "motions" to objects. Kenneth Burke, *A Grammar of Motives* (Berkeley: University of California Press, 1945), 14.

118. Ken Kolsbun with Mike Sweeney, *Peace: The Biography of a Symbol* (Washington, DC: National Geographic, 2008), 32–36. Barry Miles, *Peace: 50 Years of Protest* (Pleasantville, NY: Reader's Digest, 2008), is a fifty-year illustrated history of the use of the peace symbol from its origins in 1958 until 2008. The "peace symbol" still has iconic force. As recently as November 2012, the museum store at the National Mall entrance of the Smithsonian's National Museum of American History prominently displayed a neon version of the peace symbol, below which a variety of peace-symbol souvenirs were on sale—ballpoint pens (made in China), T-shirts, scarves, blank journals, pins, rings, coin purses, and copies of Kolsbun's *Peace*. When an interested scholar on a visit to the museum with his family asked the checkout clerk whether anyone had ever commented on or complained about the display and the neon sign, which was visible across the lobby, she answered that a few people had seemed angry about it, although it was otherwise very popular. It seemed clear that for her, it was simply a pop culture symbol from the 1960s; for old peace activists and Vietnam veterans, it was more potent. But the presumed hostility of Vietnam veterans and war protesters for each other is a complicated historical story. In 1970 there were active antiwar veterans, especially those in Vietnam Veterans Against the War, and civilian antiwar protesters seldom expressed hostility toward troops or veterans. For a history of what he interprets as a cultural and a politically manufactured myth of such conflict, see Jerry Lembcke, *The Spitting Image: Myth, Memory, and the Legacy of Vietnam* (New York: New York University Press, 1998). According to Lembcke, the myth of the spat-upon returning Vietnam veteran was invented by the first Bush administration in 1990 "to dissuade people from opposing the Gulf War" (ix). The peace symbol appeared recently in a "hippie chic" display and sale at the Boston Museum of Fine Arts, and souvenir objects with the peace symbol often decorate items on sale in grocery and convenience stores.

119. The song "Give Peace a Chance," by John Lennon, was released as a single in July 1969. The song was immensely popular in the antiwar movement.

120. Joe McGinniss, *The Selling of the President* (New York: Pocket Books, 1970); see also Timothy Crouse, *The Boys on the Bus* (New York: Random House, 1973), and Kathleen Hall Jamieson, *Packaging the Presidency: A History and Criticism of Presidential Campaign Advertising* (New York: Oxford University Press, 1984).

121. For the larger cultural context, see Susan Jeffords, *The Remasculinization of American Culture: Gender and the Vietnam War* (Bloomington: Indiana University Press, 1989).

122. The "V" sign was used in World War II, notably by British prime minister Winston Churchill, as a "V for Victory" sign. In the 1960s the peace movement adopted the "V" as a peace symbol. The raised fist is an old revolutionary, sometimes Communist, gesture. At the Mexico City Olympics in October 1968, two black American athletes, Tommie Smith and John Carlos, raised gloved fists in a "black power"—or, as they said, a "human rights"—salute at the medals ceremony. The Olympics and the US committee banned them from the Games and expelled them from the Olympic Village. The raised fist gesture also appears in plate 22, "Boycott War. Buy Peace." The fist is identified as one of one hundred ideas that changed graphic design in Steven Heller and Véronique Vienne, *100 Ideas that Changed Graphic Design* (London: Laurence King Publishing, 2012), who point out that the fist gesture was a common gesture in the American New Left and SDS, and that it had appeared in posters in both the United States and in Paris in 1968 (22–23). The "V" sign for "victory" was first proposed as a resistance symbol by Victor de Laveleye in early 1940. The sign could quickly be chalked on a wall or sidewalk, thus avoiding retribution from German occupiers; the symbol quickly spread throughout Europe. See William K. Klingaman, *1941: Our Lives in a World on the Edge* (New York: Harper and Row, 1988), 47; William Manchester and Paul Reid, *The Last Lion: Winston Spencer Churchill; Defender of the Realm, 1940–1965* (New York: Little, Brown, 2012), 274–75.

123. James T. Patterson, *Grand Expectations: The United States, 1945–1971* (New York: Oxford University Press, 1996), 656.

124. Ibid., 657. See Haig A. Bosmajian and Hamida Bosmajian, eds., *The Rhetoric of the Civil Rights Movement* (New York: Random House, 1969).

125. Drew D. Hansen, *The Dream: Martin Luther King, Jr., and the Speech that Inspired a Nation* (New York: HarperCollins, 2003), 195.

126. Simon Hall, *Peace and Freedom: The Civil Rights and Antiwar Movements in the 1960s* (Philadelphia: University of Pennsylvania Press, 2005), 186.

127. James Baldwin, "Nobody Knows My Name," in *Collected Essays* (New York: Library of America, 1998), 208.

128. Stokely Carmichael, "Black Power" (Berkeley, California, October 29, 1966), in *Words of a Century: The Top 100 American Speeches, 1900–1999*, ed. Stephen E. Lucas and Martin J. Medhurst (New York: Oxford University Press, 2009), 443.

129. Ibid., 447.

130. Curtis J. Austin observes that the Black Panther Party "stood alone among Black Power organizations in its willingness to ally with progressive whites on certain issues. Its willingness to join with and fight for a rainbow coalition of other organizations made it popular with students and different nationalities throughout the Third World." Curtis J. Austin, *Up Against the Wall: Violence in the Making and Unmaking of the Black Panther Party* (Fayetteville: University of Arkansas Press, 2006), 336. See also Donna Jean Murch, *Living for the City: Migration, Education, and the Rise of the Black Panther Party in Oakland, California* (Chapel Hill: University of North Carolina Press, 2010).

131. The cover illustration for Harvey Pekar, *Students for a Democratic Society: A Graphic History* (New York: Hill and Wang, 2008), features a cartoon showing a mixed-race, mixed-gender protest march at the White House. A raised fist is in the foreground; in the background a figure carries a sign reading "Protest Is Patriotic." The "Peace Is Patriotic" poster is reproduced in *The Poster: 1,000 Posters from Toulouse-Lautrec to Sagmeister*, ed. Cees W. de Jong, Alston W.

Purvis, and Martijn F. Le Coultre (New York: Abrams, 2010), 390.

132. The flag in plate 44 could be rotated to show the flag right side up, but then the guns (red stripes) would be upside down; when the guns are right side up, the flag is upside down.

133. See especially Adam Rome, *The Genius of Earth Day: How a 1970 Teach-In Unexpectedly Made the First Green Generation* (New York: Hill and Wang, 2013). The environmental movement soon became the focus of a new generation of scholars in the field of environmental rhetoric. See also Frank Zelko, *Make It a Green Peace! The Rise of Countercultural Environmentalism* (New York: Oxford University Press, 2013).

134. Herbert Aptheker, *One Continual Cry: David Walker's "Appeal to the Colored Citizens of the World," 1829–1830; Its Setting and Its Meaning, Together with the Full Text of the Third, and Last, Edition of the "Appeal"* (New York: Humanities Press, 1965). This edition would almost certainly have been accessible in Berkeley in 1970.

135. Sean Wilentz, ed., *David Walker's Appeal in Four Articles; Together with a Preamble, to the Coloured Citizens of the World, But in Particular, and Very Expressly, to Those of the United States of America* (New York: Hill and Wang, 1995), 75. The revised edition, edited and with an introduction by Wilentz, was originally issued in 1965. The original text, as reproduced here, inserts a pointing finger after "1776."

136. See John Louis Lucaites, "The Irony of 'Equality' in Black Abolitionist Discourse: The Case of Frederick Douglass's 'What to the Slave Is the Fourth of July?,'" in *Rhetoric and Political Culture in Nineteenth-Century America*, ed. Thomas W. Benson (East Lansing: Michigan State University Press, 1997), 47–69; and, in the same volume, James Jasinski, "Rearticulating History in Epideictic Discourse: Frederick Douglass's 'The Meaning of the Fourth of July to the Negro,'" 71–89; Martha Solomon Watson, "The Dynamics of Intertextuality: Re-reading the Declaration of Independence," 91–111; David Henry, "Garrison at Philadelphia: The 'Declaration of Sentiments' as Instrumental Rhetoric," 113–29; and

Michael C. Leff, "Lincoln Among the Nineteenth-Century Orators," 131–55.

137. Lawrence J. Prelli writes, "Rhetorics of display are nearly ubiquitous in contemporary communication and culture and, thus, have become the dominant rhetoric of our time." Lawrence J. Prelli, "Rhetorics of Display: An Introduction," in *Rhetorics of Display*, ed. Prelli (Columbia: University of South Carolina Press, 2006), 2.

138. For a brief history of Italian political posters, see Luciano Cheles, "Picture Battles in the Piazza: The Political Poster," in *The Art of Persuasion: Political Communication in Italy from 1945 to the 1990s*, ed. Luciano Cheles and Lucio Sponza (Manchester: Manchester University Press, 2002), 124–79.

139. Heller and Vienne, *100 Ideas that Changed Graphic Design*, 180.

140. Joe Austin, *Taking the Train: How Graffiti Art Became an Urban Crisis in New York City* (New York: Columbia University Press, 2001), 4. See also James Murray and Karla Murray, *Broken Windows: Graffiti NYC* (Corte Madera, CA: Gingko Press, 2002).

141. Norman Mailer, "The Faith of Graffiti," in Mervyn Kurlansky and Jon Naar, *The Faith of Graffiti* (New York: Praeger, 1974), n.p.

142. In figure 48, on the wall under the "d" in "Wanted," someone has scratched, or written in pencil, "I Love Bush."

143. Graffiti have existed in Rome since ancient times; graffiti mean differently, in cultural and rhetorical terms, according to time, place, and circumstance. Modern tourists may encounter ancient graffiti in the ruins of Pompeii, Rome, and Ostia Antica and may see graffiti scratched by Italian victims of the Nazi occupation of Rome in the former Gestapo headquarters on Via Tasso, now a museum to the resistance. See J. A. Baird and Claire Taylor, eds., *Ancient Graffiti in Context* (New York: Routledge, 2011); Stanislao G. Pugliese, *Desperate Inscriptions: Graffiti from the Nazi Prison in Rome, 1943–1944* (Boca Raton, FL: Bordighera, 2002).

144. See Gitlin, *Whole World* and *The Sixties*; Hayden, *Reunion*; Kirkpatrick Sale, *SDS* (New York: Random House, 1973); Jeremy Varon, *Bringing the War Home: The Weather*

Underground, the Red Army Faction, and Revolutionary Violence in the Sixties and Seventies (Berkeley: University of California Press, 2004).

145. A poster evidently from Berkeley, in the University of British Columbia collection, shows a menacing Richard Nixon holding a double-barrel shotgun. One barrel reads, "student dead"; the other, "Panther dead." In the upper background are the bleeding words "That'll Learn 'Em." At the bottom of the black figure of Nixon are the words, "Bring the War Home." "Bring the War Home," black and red painted print [evidently silk screen], Berkeley Poster Collection, University of British Columbia Library, Rare Books and Special Collections, UBC Identifier: Berkeley_50_247. Several much more radical, even revolutionary, posters are in the University of California Archives collection of May 1970 posters from Berkeley.

146. "Fight ROTC. Join SDS," photographic print, Berkeley Poster Collection, Rare Books and Special Collections, University of British Columbia Library, UBC Identifier: Berkeley_36_180. The poster is attributed to SDS. On May 15, 1970, an arson fire was discovered at the Berkeley ROTC building.

147. In February 2013 I traveled to Berkeley to inspect the posters in the collection of the University of California Archives on the Berkeley campus. I looked at every poster in the collection, making notes and taking reference photographs of each poster. The UC Berkeley collection may be found in the archives in a set of six oversize boxes and nine oversize folders, under the call number UC Archives ff308h. R311p. These posters, which were gathered at the time by UC librarians, archivists, and others, were arranged for the files by Lincoln Cushing. I am grateful to Cushing for his pioneering work in helping to preserve the posters and making them available for research. He generously responded to an inquiry about how to find the posters in the archive by providing me with the call number. I am also grateful to David Kessler and the staff of the UC Archives for their help. These Berkeley posters are a treasure, many of them existing, apparently, only in single, original survivals from the time—surely it is time for a benefactor to endow an effort to preserve, digitize, and render these posters accessible.

148. The Oakland Museum of California, Berkeley 1970 Workshop, http://collections.museumca.org/?q=category/subject/berkeley-1970-workshop. Some of the 183 images are alternate versions of single designs.

149. The rat motif appears in one of the 1968 Paris Atelier Populaire posters. In "Action Civique: Vermine Fasciste," a menacing rat looks over one shoulder toward the viewer. Action Civique was a pro-government right-wing political group.

150. On the use of napalm in Vietnam, its role in student protests, and its representation in cultural memory, see Robert M. Neer, *Napalm: An American Biography* (Cambridge, MA: Belknap Press, 2013).

151. University of California Archives, ff308h.R311p, Box 6, "Students for Peace. May 1970. Unite in Search of Amerika" folder.

152. Burner, *Making Peace*. For windows into a certain sort of largely silent liberal faculty member of the time, see John R. Searle, *The Campus War: A Sympathetic Look at the University in Agony* (New York: World Publishing, 1971), and Roger Rosenblatt, *Coming Apart: A Memoir of the Harvard Wars of 1969* (Boston: Little, Brown, 1997). Searle is writing from the perspective of Berkeley; Rosenblatt, from that of Harvard. Ward Just depicts the situation of a cynical antiwar congressional liberal in the title story of *The Congressman Who Loved Flaubert, and Other Washington Stories* (Boston: Little, Brown, 1973). But liberals often led the opposition to the war. See Nancy Zaroulis and Gerald Sullivan, *Who Spoke Up? American Protest Against the War in Vietnam, 1963–1975* (Garden City, NY: Doubleday, 1984). See also Marvin E. Gettleman and David Mermelstein, eds., *The Failure of American Liberalism: After the Great Society* (New York: Vintage, 1971); the book is a revised and updated version of the editors' earlier collection of essays titled *The Great Society Reader*.

153. Hariman and Lucaites, *No Caption Needed*, 19. On the intellectual and political history of late-twentieth-century fragmentation, see Daniel T. Rodgers, *Age of Fracture* (Cambridge, MA: Harvard University Press, 2011).

154. John le Carré, *The Little Drummer Girl* (New York: Alfred A. Knopf, 1983), 29–30.

155. Bryan Turner, "The 1968 Student Revolts: The Expressive Revolution and Generational Politics," in *The Disobedient Generation: Social Theorists in the Sixties*, ed. Alan Sica and Stephen P. Turner (Chicago: University of Chicago Press, 2005), 275–76.

156. See "Occupy Cal 11/9/11" by Miles Mathews, http://youtu.be/buovLQ9qyWQ. For the pepper spray incident at UC Davis, see "UC Davis Protesters Pepper Sprayed," by asucd, http://youtu.be/6AdDLhPwpp4.

157. A photograph by Stephen Shames from spring 1970, after the Cambodian incursion, shows a street protester throwing a tear gas canister back at the police. Berkeley Art Center Association, *The Whole World's Watching*, 17. The "Blue Meanies" refers to the Beatles film *Yellow Submarine* (1968).

158. Lloyd F. Bitzer and Edwin Black, foreword to *The Prospect of Rhetoric*, ed. Bitzer and Black (Englewood Cliffs, NJ: Prentice-Hall, 1971), vi.

159. There were to have been twenty-four conferees at Pheasant Run. Phillip K. Tompkins of Kent State University stayed in Ohio to help deal with the aftermath of the shootings on his campus.

160. Douglas Ehninger, Thomas W. Benson, Ernest E. Ettlich, Walter R. Fisher, Harry P. Kerr, Richard L. Larson, Raymond E. Nadeau, and Lyndrey A. Niles, "Report of the Committee on the Scope of Rhetoric and the Place of Rhetorical Studies in Higher Education," in Bitzer and Black, *Prospect of Rhetoric*, 217; Thomas O. Sloan, Richard B. Gregg, Thomas R. Nilsen, Irving J. Rein, Herbert W. Simons, Herman G. Stelzner, and Donald W. Zacharias, "Report of the Committee on the Advancement and Refinement of Rhetorical Criticism," in ibid., 220.

161. Especially useful surveys of the emergence of visual rhetoric after 1970 may be found in Lester C. Olson, Cara A. Finnegan, and Diane S. Hope, "Visual Rhetoric in Communication: Continuing Questions and Contemporary Issues," in *Visual Rhetoric: A Reader in Communication and American Culture*, ed. Olson, Finnegan, and Hope (Thousand Oaks, CA: Sage, 2008), 1–14; Diane S. Hope, "Identity and Visual Communication," in *Visual Communication: Perception, Rhetoric, and Technology*, ed. Hope (Cresskill, NJ: Hampton Press, 2006), 1–27; Prelli, "Rhetorics of Display," 1–38; and Lester C. Olson, "Intellectual and Conceptual Resources for Visual Rhetoric: A Re-examination of Scholarship Since 1950," *Review of Communication* 7, no. 1 (January 2007): 1–20. On various attempts to refound and define visual rhetoric, especially in the disciplines of communication and English, see also Charles A. Hill and Marguerite Helmers, eds., *Defining Visual Rhetorics* (New York: Routledge, 2004).

SOURCES

ARCHIVAL COLLECTIONS AND LIBRARIES

Bibliothèque nationale de France
Center for the Study of Political Graphics, Los
    Angeles
Hoover Institution, Stanford University
Imperial War Museums (United Kingdom)
Northwestern University, Digital Collections
Oakland Museum of California
    "All of Us or None" Archive Project
    (Michael Rossman)
    Berkeley 1970 Workshop Collection
Pennsylvania State University Libraries,
    Special Collections
    Thomas W. Benson Political Protest
    Collection
United States Library of Congress
United States National Archives and Records
    Administration
University of British Columbia Library, Rare
    Books and Special Collections
    Berkeley Poster Collection
University of California, Berkeley, University
    Archives
Victoria and Albert Museum
Wolfsonian Collection

BIBLIOGRAPHY

Adams, Alyssa. *Eddie Adams: Vietnam*. New
    York: Umbrage, 2008.
Agnew, Spiro. *Collected Speeches of Spiro
    Agnew*. New York: Audubon Books, 1971.
———. *Frankly Speaking: A Collection of
    Extraordinary Speeches*. Washington, DC:
    Public Affairs Press, 1970.
Anderson, Carolyn Gilpin. "Students and
    Administrators: Confrontation and
    Communication." MA thesis, Pennsylva-
    nia State University, 1972.
Anderson, Terry H. *The Movement and the
    Sixties*. New York: Oxford University
    Press, 1995.
Andresen, Lee. *Battle Notes: Music of the Viet-
    nam War*. 2nd ed. Superior, WI: Savage
    Press, 2003.
Andrews, James R. "Confrontation at Colum-
    bia: A Case Study in Coercive Rhetoric."
    Quarterly Journal of Speech 55 (1969):
    9–16.
Anreus, Alejandro, Diana L. Linden, and Jona-
    than Weinberg, eds. *The Social and the
    Real: Political Art of the 1930s in the West-
    ern Hemisphere*. University Park: Penn-
    sylvania State University Press, 2006.
Appelbaum, Stanley, ed. *The Complete "Masters
    of the Poster."* New York: Dover, 1990.
Appy, Christian G. *Patriots: The Vietnam War
    Remembered from All Sides*. New York:
    Viking, 2003.
———. *Working-Class War: American Combat
    Soldiers and Vietnam*. Chapel Hill: Uni-
    versity of North Carolina Press, 1993.
Aptheker, Herbert. *One Continual Cry: David
    Walker's "Appeal to the Colored Citizens
    of the World," 1829–1830; Its Setting*

and Its Meaning, Together with the Full Text of the Third, and Last, Edition of the "Appeal." New York: Humanities Press, 1965.

Aristotle. On Rhetoric: A Theory of Civic Discourse. Translated by George A. Kennedy. 2nd ed. New York: Oxford University Press, 2007.

Atelier Populaire. Posters from the Revolution, Paris, May, 1968: Texts and Posters. London: Dobson Books; Indianapolis: Bobbs-Merrill, 1969.

Atelier Populaire: Présenté par lui-meme; 87 affiches de mai–juin 1968. Paris: Usines Universités Union, 1968.

Aulich, James. War Posters: Weapons of Mass Communication. London: Thames and Hudson, 2007.

Austin, Curtis J. Up Against the Wall: Violence in the Making and Unmaking of the Black Panther Party. Fayetteville: University of Arkansas Press, 2006.

Austin, Joe. Taking the Train: How Graffiti Art Became an Urban Crisis in New York City. New York: Columbia University Press, 2001.

Baird, J. A., and Claire Taylor, eds. Ancient Graffiti in Context. New York: Routledge, 2011.

Baker, Steve. "Describing Images of the National Self: Popular Accounts of the Construction of Pictorial Identity in the First World War Poster." Oxford Art Journal 13, no. 2 (1990): 24–30.

Balaban, John. Remembering Heaven's Face. New York: Poseidon, 1991.

Baldwin, James. Collected Essays. New York: Library of America, 1998.

Barbero, Luca Massimo. Pittura dura: Dal graffitismo alla street art. Milan: Electa, 1999.

Barnes, Susan B. "Don't Let Him Down! WWII Propaganda Posters." In Visual Impact: The Power of Visual Persuasion, edited by Susan B. Barnes, 95–116. Cresskill, NJ: Hampton Press, 2009.

———. "Rural Electrification Administration: A Rhetorical Analysis of the Lester Beall Posters, 1937–1941." In Visual Communication: Perception, Rhetoric,

and Technology, edited by Diane S. Hope, 209–33. New York: Hampton Press, 2006.

———, ed. Visual Impact: The Power of Visual Persuasion. Cresskill, NJ: Hampton Press, 2009.

Barnicoat, John. A Concise History of Posters. London, 1972.

———. "Poster." In Grove Art Online / Oxford Art Online. Oxford University Press, accessed April 10, 2012, http://www .oxfordartonline.com/subscriber/article/ grove/art/T068980.

Barthes, Roland. Elements of Semiology. New York: Hill and Wang, 1968.

———. Mythologies. Collection "Pierres Vives." Paris: Éditions du Seuil, 1957.

———. "Rhetoric of the Image." In Image, Music, Text, translated by Stephen Heath, 32–51. New York: Hill and Wang, 1977.

Bennett, Jill. Empathic Vision: Affect, Trauma, and Contemporary Art. Stanford: Stanford University Press, 2005.

Benson, Thomas W., ed. American Rhetoric: Context and Criticism. Carbondale: Southern Illinois University Press, 1989.

———, ed. American Rhetoric in the New Deal Era, 1932–1945. East Lansing: Michigan State University Press, 2006.

———. "Another Shooting in Cowtown." Quarterly Journal of Speech 67 (1981): 347–406.

———. "The Cornell School of Rhetoric: Idiom and Institution." Communication Quarterly 51 (2003): 1–56.

———. "Edwin Black's Cornell University." Rhetoric and Public Affairs 10 (2007): 481–88.

———. "Implicit Communication Theory in Campaign Coverage." In Television Coverage of the 1980 Presidential Campaign, edited by William C. Adams, 103–16. Norwood, NJ: Ablex Publishing, 1983.

———. "Joe: An Essay in the Rhetorical Criticism of Film." Journal of Popular Culture (Winter 1974): 610–18.

———. "Looking for the Public in the Popular: Collective Memory and the Hollywood Blacklist." In The Terministic Screen: Rhetorical Perspectives on Film, edited by

David Blakesley, 129–45. Carbondale: Southern Illinois University Press, 2003.

———. "Look! Rhetoric!" In *Visual Rhetoric: A Reader in Communication and American Culture,* edited by Lester C. Olson, Cara A. Finnegan, and Diane S. Hope, 413–16. Thousand Oaks, CA: Sage, 2008.

———. "Rhetoric and Autobiography: The Case of Malcolm X." *Quarterly Journal of Speech,* 60 (1974): 1–13.

———, ed. *Rhetoric and Political Culture in Nineteenth-Century America.* East Lansing: Michigan State University Press, 1997.

———. "Rhetoric as a Way of Being." In *American Rhetoric: Context and Criticism,* edited by Thomas W. Benson, 293–322. Carbondale: Southern Illinois University Press, 1989.

———. "The Senses of Rhetoric: A Topical System for Critics." *Central States Speech Journal* 29 (1978): 237–50.

———, ed. *Speech Communication in the 20th Century.* Carbondale: Southern Illinois University Press, 1989.

———. " 'To Lend a Hand': Gerald Ford, Watergate, and the White House Speechwriters." *Rhetoric and Public Affairs* 1 (1998): 201–25.

———. "Violence: Communication Breakdown?" *Today's Speech* 18 (Winter 1970): 39–46.

———. *Writing JFK: Presidential Rhetoric and the Press in the Bay of Pigs Crisis.* College Station: Texas A&M University Press, 2003.

Benson, Thomas W., and Carolyn Anderson. *Reality Fictions: The Films of Frederick Wiseman.* 2nd ed. Carbondale: Southern Illinois University Press, 2002.

Benson, Thomas W., and Kenneth Frandsen. *An Orientation to Nonverbal Communication.* Palo Alto, CA: Science Research Associates, 1976.

Benson, Thomas W., and Bonnie Johnson. "The Rhetoric of Resistance: Confrontation with the Warmakers, Washington, DC, October 1967." *Today's Speech* 16 (September 1968): 35–42. Reprinted, with photographs by T. W. Benson, in *Colleague* 5 (March/April 1969): 9–14.

Benson, Thomas W., and Brian J. Snee, eds. *The Rhetoric of the New Political Documentary.* Carbondale: Southern Illinois University Press, 2008.

Berger, Maurice. *Representing Vietnam, 1965– 1973: The Antiwar Movement in America.* New York: The Bertha and Karl Leubsdorf Art Gallery, 1988.

Berkeley Art Center Association. *The Whole World's Watching: Peace and Social Justice Movements of the 1960s and 1970s.* Berkeley, CA: Berkeley Art Center Association, 2001.

Berrigan, Daniel. *The Trial of the Catonsville Nine.* Boston: Beacon Press, 1970.

Bestley, Russell, and Ian Noble. *Up Against the Wall: International Poster Design.* Mies, Switzerland: RotoVision, 2002.

Bird, William L., Jr., and Harry R. Rubenstein. *Design for Victory: World War II Posters on the American Home Front.* New York: Princeton Architectural Press, 1998.

Bishop, Claire, ed. *Participation.* Cambridge, MA: MIT Press, 2006.

Bitzer, Lloyd F., and Edwin R. Black, eds. *The Prospect of Rhetoric.* Report of the National Developmental Project, sponsored by the Speech Communication Association. Englewood Cliffs, NJ: Prentice-Hall, 1971.

Black, Edwin R. *Rhetorical Criticism: A Study in Method.* New York: Macmillan, 1965.

Blakesley, David. *The Terministic Screen: Rhetorical Perspectives on Film.* Carbondale: Southern Illinois University Press, 2007.

Bloom, Alexander, and Wini Breines. *"Takin' It to the Streets": A Sixties Reader.* 3rd ed. New York: Oxford University Press, 2010.

Bosmajian, Haig A., and Hamida Bosmajian, eds. *The Rhetoric of the Civil Rights Movement.* New York: Random House, 1969.

Bostwick, William. "Rock Versus Paper." *Print* 66, no. 1 (February 2012): 52–59.

Bourget, P. *Sur les Murs de Paris et des France.* (Paris, 1980).

Brown, Josh, and Ellen Noonan. "Calls to Action: Posters of the Anti-Vietnam War Movement." *Radical History Review*

2000, no. 78 (September 2000): 141–48.

Brown, Sam, and Len Ackland. *Why Are We Still in Vietnam?* New York: Random House, 1970.

Browne, Stephen Howard. "Rhetorical Criticism and the Challenges of Bilateral Argument." *Philosophy and Rhetoric* 40 (2007): 108–18.

Bryan-Wilson, Julia. *Art Workers: Radical Practice in the Vietnam War Era.* Berkeley: University of California Press, 2009.

Buckley, Kerry W. "A President for the 'Great Silent Majority': Bruce Barton's Construction of Calvin Coolidge." *New England Quarterly* 76, no. 4 (December 2003): 593–626.

Bumgardner, Georgia B. *American Broadsides.* Barre, MA: Imprint Society, 1971.

Burke, Kenneth. *A Grammar of Motives.* Berkeley: University of California Press, 1945.

Burner, David. *Making Peace with the 60s.* Princeton: Princeton University Press, 1996.

Burridge, Joseph. "Hunting Is Not Just for Blood-Thirsty Toffs: The Countryside Alliance and the Visual Rhetoric of a Poster Campaign." *Text and Talk* 28, no. 1 (January 2008): 31–53.

Bustard, Bruce I. *A New Deal for the Arts.* Washington, DC, and Seattle, WA: National Archives and Records Administration in association with the University of Washington Press, 1997.

Campbell, Karlyn Kohrs. "'Conventional Wisdom—Traditional Form': A Rejoinder." *Quarterly Journal of Speech* 58 (1972): 451–55.

———. *Critiques of Contemporary Rhetoric.* Belmont, CA: Wadsworth, 1972.

———. "An Exercise in the Rhetoric of Mythical America." In *Critiques of Contemporary Rhetoric,* 50–58. Belmont, CA: Wadsworth, 1972.

———. Review of *Criticism of Oral Rhetoric,* by Carroll C. Arnold. *Today's Speech* 22 (Summer 1974): 39–41.

Camus, Albert. *Resistance, Rebellion, and Death.* New York: Vintage, 1995.

Cannon, Lou. *Governor Reagan: His Rise to Power.* New York: PublicAffairs, 2003.

Caputo, Philip. *A Rumor of War.* New York: Henry Holt, 1996.

Carpenter, Ronald H., and Robert V. Seltzer. "Nixon, *Patton,* and a Silent Majority Sentiment About the Viet Nam War: The Cinematographic Bases of a Rhetorical Stance." *Central States Speech Journal* 25 (Summer 1974): 105–10.

Carter, Ennis. *Posters for the People: Art of the WPA.* Philadelphia: Quirk Books, 2008.

Cartwright, Lisa, and Stephen Mandiberg. "Obama and Shepard Fairey: The Copy and Political Iconography in the Age of the Demake." *Journal of Visual Culture* 8, no. 2 (2009): 172–76.

Cheles, Luciano. "Picture Battles in the Piazza: The Political Poster." In *The Art of Persuasion: Political Communication in Italy from 1945 to the 1990s,* edited by Luciano Cheles and Lucio Sponza, 124–79. Manchester: Manchester University Press, 2002.

Clark, Gregory. *Rhetorical Landscapes in America: Variations on a Theme from Kenneth Burke.* Columbia: University of South Carolina Press, 2004.

Clecak, Peter. *Radical Paradoxes: Dilemmas of the American Left, 1945–1970.* New York: Harper and Row, 1973.

Cloud, Dana L. "'To Veil the Threat of Terror': Afghan Women and the 'Clash of Civilizations' in the Imagery of the U.S. War on Terrorism." *Quarterly Journal of Speech* 83 (1997): 289–310.

Cohen, Allen, and Ronald L. Filippelli. *Times of Sorrow and Hope: Documenting Everyday Life in Pennsylvania During the Depression and World War II.* University Park: Pennsylvania State University Press, 2003.

Cohen, Robert. *Freedom's Orator: Mario Savio and the Radical Legacy of the 1960s.* New York: Oxford University Press, 2009.

Cohen, Robert, and Reginald E. Zelnick, eds. *The Free Speech Movement: Reflections on Berkeley in the 1960s.* Berkeley: University of California Press, 2002.

Collins, Bradford R. "The Poster as Art; Jules Chéret and the Struggle for the Equality of the Arts in Late Nineteenth-Century France." *Design Issues* 2, no. 1 (Spring, 1985): 41–50.

Copeland, Alan, Nikki Arai, and Berkeley Phoenix Gallery. *People's Park.* New York: Ballantine Books, 1969.

Cowie, Jefferson R. *Stayin' Alive: The 1970s and the Last Days of the Working Class.* New York: New Press, 2010.

Crouse, Timothy. *The Boys on the Bus.* New York: Random House, 1973.

Cushing, Lincoln. *Agitate! Educate! Organize! American Labor Posters.* Ithaca, NY: ILR Press, 2009.

———. *All of Us or None: Social Justice Posters of the San Francisco Bay Area.* Berkeley, CA: Heyday, 2012.

———. Review of *4973: Berkeley Protest Posters 1970.* (2008). http://www.docspopuli.org/articles/4973Review.html.

———. *Revolucion! Cuban Poster Art.* San Francisco: Chronicle Books, 2003.

Cushing, Lincoln, and Ann Tompkins. *Chinese Posters: Art from the Great Proletarian Cultural Revolution.* San Francisco: Chronicle Books, 2007.

Dallek, Matthew. "Liberalism Overthrown." *American Heritage* 47, no. 6 (October 1996): 39.

D'Angelo, Frank J. "Sacred Cows Make Great Hamburgers: The Rhetoric of Graffiti." *College Composition and Communication* 25, no. 2 (May 1974): 173–80.

Dary, Anne. *Les Affiches de Mai 1968.* Paris: Beaux-Arts de Paris, 2008.

Davies, Peter. *The Truth About Kent State: A Challenge to the American Conscience.* New York: Farrar, Straus and Giroux, 1973.

DeBenedetti, Charles. *An American Ordeal: The Antiwar Movement of the Vietnam Era.* Syracuse: Syracuse University Press, 1990.

Debord, Guy. "Report on the Construction of Situations and on the International Situationist Tendency's Conditions of Organization and Action [1957]." In *Situationist International Anthology,* translated by Ken Knabb, 25–43. Revised and expanded. Berkeley, CA: Bureau of Public Secrets, 2006.

———. *Society of the Spectacle.* Detroit: Black and Red, 1983.

de Jong, Cees W., Alston W. Purvis, and Martijn F. Le Coultre. *The Poster: 1,000 Posters from Toulouse-Lautrec to Sagmeister.* New York: Abrams, 2010.

DeLuca, Kevin Michael. *Image Politics: The New Rhetoric of Environmental Activism.* New York: Guilford, 1999.

DeNoon, Christopher. *Posters of the WPA.* Los Angeles: Wheatley Press, 1987.

Denton, Robert E., Jr. "The Rhetorical Functions of Slogans: Classifications and Characteristics." *Communication Quarterly* 28, no. 2 (Spring 1980): 10–18.

DeRoo, Rebecca J. *The Museum Establishment and Contemporary Art: The Politics of Artistic Display in France After 1968.* New York: Cambridge University Press, 2006.

Dumitrescu, Delia. "Know Me, Love Me, Fear Me: The Anatomy of Candidate Poster Designs in the 2007 French Legislative Elections." *Political Communication* 27, no. 1 (March 2010): 20–43.

Dunaway, Finis. "Gas Masks, Pogo, and the Ecological Indian: Earth Day and the Visual Politics of American Environmentalism." *American Quarterly* 60, no. 1 (March 2008): 67–99.

Dundes, Alan. *Analytic Essays in Folklore.* The Hague: Mouton, 1975.

Eck, Caroline van. *Classical Rhetoric and the Visual Arts in Early Modern Europe.* New York: Cambridge University Press, 2007.

Edelman, Murray. *Politics as Symbolic Action: Mass Arousal and Quiescence.* New York: Academic Press, 1971.

Engels, Jeremy. Review of *Dissent from War,* by Robert L. Ivie. *Quarterly Journal of Speech* 94 (2008): 234–38.

Eskilson, Stephen J. *Graphic Design: A New History.* New Haven: Yale University Press, 2007.

Fall, Bernard. *Street Without Joy.* Mechanicsburg, PA: Stackpole Books, 1961.

———. *The Two Viet-Nams: A Political and Military Analysis.* 2nd ed. New York: Praeger, 1967.

Farber, David. *Chicago '68.* Chicago: University of Chicago Press, 1988.

————, ed. *The Sixties*. Chapel Hill: University of North Carolina Press, 1994.

Feenberg, Andrew, and Jim Freedman. *When Poetry Ruled the Streets: The French May Events of 1968*. Albany: State University of New York Press, 2001.

Ferstle, Thomas. *Assessing Visual Rhetoric—Problems, Practices and Possible Solutions*. Saarbrücken, Germany: VDM Publishing, 2007.

Fink, Carole, Philipp Gassert, and Detlef Junker, eds. *1968: The World Transformed*. New York: Cambridge University Press, 1998.

Finnegan, Cara A. *Picturing Poverty: Print Culture and FSA Photographs*. Washington, DC: Smithsonian Institution Scholarly Press, 2003.

————. Review of *No Caption Needed: Iconic Photographs, Public Culture, and Liberal Democracy*, by Robert Hariman and John Louis Lucaites. *Rhetoric Society Quarterly* 40 (2010): 94–97.

————. "Studying Visual Modes of Public Address: Lewis Hine's Progressive-Era Child Labor Rhetoric." In *The Handbook of Rhetoric and Public Address*, edited by Shawn J. Parry-Giles and J. Michael Hogan, 250–70. West Sussex, UK: Wiley-Blackwell, 2010.

FitzGerald, Frances. *Fire in the Lake: The Vietnamese and the Americans in Vietnam*. New York: Little, Brown, 2002.

Flamm, Michael W., and David Steigerwald. *Debating the 1960s: Liberal, Conservative, and Radical Perspectives*. Lanham, MD: Rowman and Littlefield, 2008.

Fleckenstein, Kristie S., Sue Hum, and Linda T. Calendrillo, eds. *Ways of Seeing, Ways of Speaking: The Integration of Rhetoric and Vision in Constructing the Real*. West Lafayette, IN: Parlor Press, 2007.

Fleming, David. *From Form to Meaning: Freshman Composition and the Long Sixties, 1957–1974*. Pittsburgh, PA: University of Pittsburgh Press, 2011.

Foley, Michael S. *Confronting the War Machine: Draft Resistance During the Vietnam War*. Chapel Hill: University of North Carolina Press, 2003.

Ford, Simon. *Situationist International: A User's Guide*. London: Black Dog Publishing, 2004.

Foster, John. *Masters of Poster Design: Poster Design for the Next Century*. Gloucester, MA: Rockport Publishers, 2006.

Franklin, H. Bruce. *The Vietnam War in American Stories, Songs, and Poems*. Boston: Bedford/St. Martin's Press, 1996.

Frascina, Francis. *Art, Politics, and Dissent: Aspects of the Art Left in Sixties America*. Manchester: Manchester University Press, 1999.

Gallagher, Victoria, and Kelly Martin. Review of *Visual Rhetoric: A Reader in Communication and American Culture*," edited by Lester C. Olson, Cara A. Finnegan, and Diane S. Hope, eds. *Southern Communication Journal* 75, no. 5 (December 2010): 547–51.

Gallant, Mavis. *Paris Notebooks: Essays and Reviews*. New York: Random House, 1986.

Gallo, Max. *The Poster in History*. New York: W. W. Norton, 2000.

Garfinkle, Adam. *Telltale Hearts: The Origins and Impact of the Vietnam Antiwar Movement*. New York: St. Martin's Press, 1995.

Geismar, Tom, Sagi Haviv, and Ivan Chermayeff. *Identify: Basic Principles of Identity Design in the Iconic Trademarks of Chermayeff and Geismar*. New York: Print Publishing, 2011.

Gettleman, Marvin E., Jane Franklin, Marilyn B. Young, and H. Bruce Franklin, eds. *Vietnam and America: A Documented History*. New York: Grove Press, 1995.

Gettleman, Marvin E., and David Mermelstein, eds. *The Failure of American Liberalism: After the Great Society*. New York: Vintage, 1971.

Ginzburg, Carlo. "'Your Country Needs You': A Case Study in Political Iconography." *History Workshop Journal*, no. 52 (Autumn 2001): vi and 1–22.

Gitlin, Todd. *The Sixties: Years of Hope, Days of Rage*. New York: Bantam Books, 1987.

————. *The Whole World Is Watching: Mass Media in the Making and Unmaking of the New Left*. Berkeley: University of California Press, 1980.

Glaser, Milton and Mirko Ilić. *The Design of Dissent*. Gloucester, MA: Rockport Publishers, 2005.

Gombrich, E. H. *The Story of Art*. 12th ed. London: Phaidon Press, 1972.

Gordon, William A. *The Fourth of May: Killings and Coverups at Kent State*. Buffalo, NY: Prometheus Books, 1990.

Grant, Ulysses S. *Memoirs and Selected Letters*. New York: Library of America, 1990.

Gray, David A. "New Uses for Old Photos: Renovating FSA Photographs in World War II Posters." *American Studies* 47, no. 3/4 (October 2006): 5–34.

Gregg, Richard B. "The Ego-Function of the Rhetoric of Protest." *Philosophy and Rhetoric* 4, no. 2 (Spring 1971): 71–91.

Grushkin, Paul. *The Art of Classic Rock*. New York: HarperCollins, 2010.

Grushkin, Paul, and Dennis King. *Art of Modern Rock: The Poster Explosion*. San Francisco: Chronicle Books, 2004.

Halberstam, David. *The Best and the Brightest*. New York: Random House, 1972.

Hall, Mitchell. "Unsell the War: Vietnam and Antiwar Advertising." *Historian* 58, no. 1 (September 1995): 69–86.

Hall, Simon. *Peace and Freedom: The Civil Rights and Antiwar Movements in the 1960s*. Philadelphia: University of Pennsylvania Press, 2005.

———. *Rethinking the American Anti-war Movement*. New York: Routledge, 2011.

Hambourg, Serge. *Protest in Paris 1968: Photographs by Serge Hambourg*. Hanover, NH: Hood Museum of Art, Dartmouth College, 2006.

Hammond, William M. *Reporting Vietnam: Media and Military at War*. Lawrence: University Press of Kansas, 1998.

Hansen, Drew D. *The Dream: Martin Luther King, Jr., and the Speech that Inspired a Nation*. New York: HarperCollins, 2003.

Hariman, Robert, and John Louis Lucaites. *No Caption Needed: Iconic Photographs, Public Culture, and Liberal Democracy*. Chicago: University of Chicago Press, 2007.

Haskins, Ekaterina V., and James P. Zappen. "Totalitarian Visual 'Monologue': Reading Soviet Posters with Bakhtin." *RSQ: Rhetoric Society Quarterly* 40, no. 4 (Fall 2010): 326–59.

Hayden, Tom. *The Port Huron Statement: The Visionary Call of the 1960s Revolution*. New York: Thunder's Mouth Press, 2005.

———. *Reunion: A Memoir*. New York: Random House, 1988.

———. *Trial*. New York: Holt, Rinehart and Winston, 1970.

Haynie, Charles A. *A Memoir of the New Left: The Political Autobiography of Charles A. Haynie*. Edited by Aeron Haynie and Timothy S. Miller. Knoxville, TN: University of Tennessee Press, 2009.

Heideking, Jürgen, Jörg Helbig, and Anke Ortlepp, eds. *The Sixties Revisited: Culture, Society, Politics*. Heidelberg, Germany: C. Winter, 2001.

Heineman, Kenneth J. *Campus Wars: The Peace Movement at American State Universities in the Vietnam Era*. New York: New York University Press, 1993.

Heller, Steven. "Visuals." *New York Times*, December 2, 2011.

Heller, Steven, and Lita Talarico. *Design School Confidential: Extraordinary Class Projects from the International Design Schools, Colleges, and Institutes*. Gloucester, MA: Rockport Publishers, 2009.

Heller, Steven, and Véronique Vienne. *Citizen Designer: Perspectives on Design Responsibility*. New York: Allworth Press, 2003.

———. *100 Ideas that Changed Graphic Design*. London: Laurence King Publishing, 2012.

Herr, Michael. *Dispatches*. New York: Avon, 1978.

Heyman, Therese Thau. *Posters American Style*. Washington, DC: National Museum of Art, Smithsonian Institution, 1998.

Hilden, Patricia J. "The Rhetoric and Iconography of Reform: Women Coal Miners in Belgium, 1840–1914." *The Historical Journal* 34, no. 2 (June 1991): 411–36.

Hill, Charles A., and Marguerite Helmers, eds. *Defining Visual Rhetorics*. New York: Routledge, 2004.

Hill, Forbes. "Conventional Wisdom— Traditional Form—The President's

Message of November 3, 1969." *Quarterly Journal of Speech* 58, no. 4 (December 1972): 373–86.

Hoffman, Abbie, et al. *The Conspiracy*. New York: Dell, 1969.

Hoffman, Paul. *Moratorium: An American Protest*. New York: Tower, 1970.

Hope, Diane S., ed. *Visual Communication: Perception, Rhetoric, and Technology*. Cresskill, NJ: Hampton Press, 2006.

Hunt, Andrew E. *The Turning: A History of Vietnam Veterans Against the War*. New York: New York University Press, 1999.

Hylton, Cal, and Barbara Bradley. "Special Reports: Attitudes and Beliefs: The Campus Versus the Silent Majority." *Central States Speech Journal* 22, no. 1 (Spring 1971): 58–60.

Irwin, Jacqueline. "The Guilt in 'Mom, We're Home!': The Content, Control, and Critique of Modern War Protest Posters." In *Conference Papers—International Communication Association*, 1. Washington, DC: International Communication Association, 2007.

Israel, Matthew. *Kill for Peace: American Artists Against the Vietnam War*. Austin: University of Texas Press, 2013.

Isserman, Maurice, and Michael Kazin. *America Divided: The Civil War of the 1960s*. 4th ed. New York: Oxford University Press, 2012.

Ivie, Robert L. *Dissent from War*. Bloomfield, CT: Kumarian Press, 2007.

Ivins, William M., Jr. *Prints and Visual Communication*. Cambridge, MA: Harvard University Press, 1953.

James, Pearl, ed. *Picture This: World War I Posters and Visual Culture*. Lincoln: University of Nebraska Press, 2009.

Jamieson, Kathleen Hall. *Packaging the Presidency: A History and Criticism of Presidential Campaign Advertising*. New York: Oxford University Press, 1984.

Jeffords, Susan. *The Remasculinization of American Culture: Gender and the Vietnam War*. Bloomington: Indiana University Press, 1989.

Jenkins, Philip. *Decade of Nightmares: The End of the Sixties and the Making of Eighties*

America. New York: Oxford University Press, 2006.

Johnstone, Henry W., Jr. "The Philosophical Basis of Rhetoric." *Philosophy and Rhetoric* 40, no. 1 (2007): 15–26.

Jones, Bryn, and Mike O'Donnell, eds. *Sixties Radicalism and Social Movement Activism: Retreat or Resurgence?* London: Anthem Press, 2010.

Jones, Kevin T., Kenneth S. Zagacki, and Todd V. Lewis. "Communication, Liminality, and Hope: The September 11th Missing Person Posters." *Communication Studies* 58, no. 1 (March 2007): 105–21.

Jowett, Garth S., and Victoria O'Donnell. *Propaganda and Persuasion*. 4th ed. Thousand Oaks, CA: Sage, 2006.

Joyce, Robert. *The Esthetic Animal: Man, the Art-Created Art Creator*. Hicksville, NY: Exposition Press, 1975.

Juravich, Tom. "Representing Labor." *Work and Occupations* 38, no. 2 (May 2011): 143–48.

Just, Ward. *The Congressman Who Loved Flaubert, and Other Washington Stories*. Boston: Little, Brown, 1973.

———. *To What End: Report from Vietnam*. Boston: Houghton Mifflin, 1968.

Kahin, George McTurnan. *Intervention: How America Became Involved in Vietnam*. New York: Alfred A. Knopf, 1986.

Kahn, Roger. *The Battle for Morningside Heights: Why Students Rebel*. New York: William Morrow and Company, 1970.

Kaplan, Geoff, ed. *Power to the People: The Graphic Design of the Radical Press and the Rise of the Counter-Culture, 1964–1974*. Chicago: University of Chicago Press, 2013.

Karnow, Stanley. *Vietnam: A History*. New York: Penguin, 1991.

Kaufman, Michael T. *1968*. New York: Roaring Brook Press, 2009.

Kennedy, David M. *Freedom from Fear: The American People in Depression and War, 1929–1945*. New York: Oxford University Press, 1999.

Kennedy, John F. *Profiles in Courage*. New York: HarperCollins, 1964.

Kennedy, Roger G., and David Larkin. *When Art Worked: The New Deal, Art, and Democracy*. New York: Rizzoli, 2009.

Kimble, James J., and Lester C. Olson. "Visual Rhetoric Representing Rosie the Riveter: Myth and Misconception in J. Howard Miller's 'We Can Do It!' Poster." *Rhetoric and Public Affairs* 9, no. 4 (Winter 2006): 533–69.

Kitchell, Mark. *Berkeley in the Sixties.* Kitchell Films: 117 minutes, 1990.

Klimke, Martin, and Joachim Scharloth, eds. *1968 in Europe: A History of Protest and Activism, 1956–1977.* New York: Palgrave Macmillan, 2008.

Klingaman, William K. *1941: Our Lives in a World on the Edge.* New York: Harper and Row, 1988.

Knabb, Ken. *Situationist International Anthology.* Revised and expanded. Berkeley, CA: Bureau of Public Secrets, 2007.

Kolsbun, Ken, with Mike Sweeney. *Peace: The Biography of a Symbol.* Washington, DC: National Geographic, 2008.

Kress, Gunther, and Theo van Leeuwen. *Reading Images: The Grammar of Visual Design.* 2nd ed. London: Routledge, 2006.

Kugelberg, Johan, and Philippe Vermès, eds. *Beauty Is in the Street: A Visual Record of the May '68 Paris Uprising.* London: Four Corners Books, 2011.

Kunzle, David. *American Posters of Protest, 1966–70: Art as a Political Weapon.* New York: New School Art Center, 1971.

———. *L'Era di Johnson: Manifesti della gioventù studentesca e pacifista americana.* Milan: La Pietra, 1968.

———. *Posters of Protest: The Posters of Political Satire in the U.S., 1966–1970.* Santa Barbara: University of California Press, 1971.

Kurlansky, Mervyn, and Jon Naar. *The Faith of Graffiti.* New York: Praeger, 1974.

le Carré, John. *The Little Drummer Girl.* New York: Alfred A. Knopf, 1983.

———. *A Small Town in Germany.* New York: Charles Scribner's Sons, 2002.

Lefebvre, Henri. *The Explosion: Marxism and the French Revolution of May 1968.* New York: Monthly Review Press, 1969.

Lembcke, Jerry. *The Spitting Image: Myth, Memory, and the Legacy of Vietnam.* New York: New York University Press, 1998.

Lemke, Gayle, and Jacaeber Kastor. *The Art of the Fillmore, 1966–1971.* New York: Thunder's Mouth Press, 1997.

Levine, Lawrence W., and Cornelia R. Levine. *The Fireside Conversations: America Responds to FDR During the Great Depression.* Berkeley: University of California Press, 2010.

Levine, Robert A. "The Silent Majority: Neither Simple nor Simple-Minded." *Public Opinion Quarterly* 35, no. 4 (1971): 571–77.

Levy, Peter B. *The New Left and Labor in the 1960s.* Urbana: University of Illinois Press, 1994.

Lewis, Penny. *Hardhats, Hippies, and Hawks: The Vietnam Antiwar Movement as Myth and Memory.* Ithaca: Cornell University Press, 2013.

Lima, Manuel. *Visual Complexity: Mapping Patterns of Information.* New York: Princeton Architectural Press, 2011.

Lionnet, Françoise. "Immigration, Poster Art, and Transgressive Citizenship: France 1968–1988." *SubStance* 24, no. 1/2 (January 1995): 93–108.

Lippard, Lucy R. *A Different War: Vietnam in Art.* Seattle, WA: Whatcom Museum of History and Art and Real Comet Press, 1990.

Logevall, Fredrik. *Choosing War: The Lost Chance for Peace and the Escalation of War in Vietnam.* Berkeley, CA: University of California Press, 1999.

———. *Embers of War: The Fall of an Empire and the Making of America's Vietnam.* New York: Random House, 2012.

Low, Seth, and Neil Smith, eds. *The Politics of Public Space.* New York: Routledge, 2006.

Lucas, Stephen E., and Martin J. Medhurst, eds. *Words of a Century: The Top 100 American Speeches, 1900–1999.* New York: Oxford University Press, 2009.

Lytle, Mark Hamilton. *America's Uncivil Wars: The Sixties Era from Elvis to the Fall of Richard Nixon.* New York: Oxford University Press, 2006.

Mailer, Norman. *The Armies of the Night: History as a Novel, the Novel as History.* New York: New American Library, 1968.

Manchester, William, and Paul Reid. *The Last Lion: Winston Spencer Churchill; Defender of the Realm, 1940–1965*. New York: Little, Brown, 2012.

Manchette, Jean-Patrick. *Fatale*. New York: NYRB Classics, 2011.

———. *Three to Kill*. San Francisco, CA: City Lights Publishers, 2002.

Mann, James, ed. *Peace Signs: The Anti-war Movement Illustrated*. Zurich: Edition Olms, 2004.

Maraniss, David. *They Marched into Sunlight: War and Peace in Vietnam and America, October 1967*. New York: Simon and Schuster, 2003.

Margolin, Victor. "Rebellion, Reform, and Revolution: American Graphic Design for Social Change." *Design Issues* 5, no. 1 (October 1988): 59–70.

Martin, Susan, ed. *Decade of Protest: Political Posters from the United States, Viet Nam, Cuba, 1965–1975*. Santa Monica, CA: Smart Art Press, 1996.

Mastrangelo, Lisa. "World War I, Public Intellectuals, and the Four Minute Men: Convergent Ideals of Public Speaking and Civic Participation." *Rhetoric and Public Affairs* 12, no. 4 (Winter 2009): 607–33.

Mattson, Kevin. *Intellectuals in Action: The Origins of the New Left and Radical Liberalism, 1945–1970*. University Park: Pennsylvania State University Press, 2002.

Mayor, A. Hyatt. *Prints and People: A Social History of Printed Pictures*. New York: The Metropolitan Museum of Art, 1971.

McAlister, John T., Jr., and Paul Mus. *The Vietnamese and Their Revolution*. New York: Harper Torchbooks, 1970.

McGinniss, Joe. *The Selling of the President*. New York: Pocket Books, 1970.

McLuhan, Marshall. *The Mechanical Bride: Folklore of Industrial Man*. New York: Vanguard Press, 1951.

Medeiros, Walter. "Mapping San Francisco, 1965–1967: Roots and Florescence of the San Francisco Counterculture." In *Summer of Love: Psychedelic Art, Social Crisis, and Counterculture in the 1960s*,

edited by Christoph Grunenberg and Jonathan Harris, 303–48. Liverpool: Liverpool University Press, 2005.

Medhurst, Martin J., ed. *Beyond the Rhetorical Presidency*. College Station: Texas A&M University Press, 1996.

Medhurst, Martin J., and Thomas W. Benson. "*The City*: The Rhetoric of Rhythm." *Communication Monographs* 48, no. 1 (March 1981): 54–72.

———, eds. *Rhetorical Dimensions in Media: A Critical Casebook*. Dubuque, IA: Kendall-Hunt, 1984.

Meggs, Philip B., and Alston W. Purvis. *Meggs' History of Graphic Design*. 4th ed. Hoboken, NJ: John Wiley and Sons, 2006.

Messaris, Paul. "Review Essay: What's Visual About 'Visual Rhetoric'?" *Quarterly Journal of Speech* 95, no. 2 (May 2009): 210–223.

Miles, Barry. *4973: Berkeley Protest Posters 1970*. London: Francis Boutle Publishers: Maggs Brothers, [2008].

———. *Peace: 50 Years of Protest*. Pleasantville, NY: Reader's Digest, 2008.

Miller, James. *"Democracy Is in the Streets": From Port Huron to the Siege of Chicago*. New York: Simon and Schuster, 1987.

Mitchell, W. J. T. *What Do Pictures Want? The Lives and Loves of Images*. Chicago: University of Chicago Press, 2006.

Moist, Kevin Michael. "A Grounded Situational Assessment of Meanings Emerging from the Consideration of Psychedelic Rock Concert Posters as a Form of Subcultural Visionary Rhetoric." PhD diss., University of Iowa, 2000.

Moore, Colin. *Propaganda Prints*. London: A&C Black, 2010.

Morone, James A. "The Struggle for American Culture." *PS: Political Science and Politics* 29, no. 3 (September 1996): 425–30.

Morris, Charles E., III, and Stephen H. Browne, eds.. *Readings on the Rhetoric of Social Protest*. 2nd ed. State College, PA: Strata Publishing, 2006.

Moser, Richard R. *The New Winter Soldiers: GI and Veteran Dissent During the Vietnam*

Era. New Brunswick: Rutgers University Press, 1996.

Mouffe, Chantal. *The Democratic Paradox.* London: Verso Books, 2005.

Müller-Brockmann, Josef, and Shizuko Yoshikawa. *Geschichte des Plakates. Histoire de L'affiche.* Zurich: ABC-Verlag, 1971.

Murch, Donna Jean. *Living for the City: Migration, Education, and the Rise of the Black Panther Party in Oakland, California.* Chapel Hill: University of North Carolina Press, 2010.

Murray, James, and Karla Murray. *Broken Windows: Graffiti NYC.* Corte Madera, CA: Gingko Press, 2002.

Myrus, Donald, ed. *Law and Disorder: The Chicago Convention and Its Aftermath.* Chicago: Donald Myrus and Burton Joseph, 1968.

Neer, Robert M. *Napalm: An American Biography.* Cambridge, MA: Belknap Press, 2013.

Newman, Robert P. "Under the Veneer: Nixon's Vietnam Speech of November 3, 1969." *Quarterly Journal of Speech* 56, no. 2 (1970): 168–78.

O'Brien, Tim. *Going After Cacciato.* New York: Delacorte, 1978.

———. *If I Die in a Combat Zone: Box Me Up and Ship Me Home.* New York: Delacorte Press, 1973.

———. *The Things They Carried.* Boston: Houghton Mifflin, 1990.

O'Connell, P. J. *The Year Behind . . . and the Year Ahead.* University Park, PA: WPSX TV, The Pennsylvania State University, 1969.

Oliver, Kendrick. *The My Lai Massacre in American History and Memory.* Manchester: Manchester University Press, 2006.

Olson, Lester C. "Benjamin Franklin's Commemorative Medal *Libertas Americana*: A Study in Rhetorical Iconology." *Quarterly Journal of Speech* 76, no. 1 (February 1990): 23–45.

———. "Benjamin Franklin's Pictorial Representations of the British Colonies in America: A Study in Rhetorical Iconol-

ogy." *Quarterly Journal of Speech* 73, no. 1 (February 1987): 18–32.

———. *Benjamin Franklin's Vision of American Community: A Study in Rhetorical Iconology.* Columbia: University of South Carolina Press, 2004.

———. *Emblems of American Community in the Revolutionary Era: A Study in Rhetorical Iconology.* Washington, DC: Smithsonian Institution Press, 1991.

———. "Intellectual and Conceptual Resources for Visual Rhetoric: A Reexamination of Scholarship Since 1950." *Review of Communication* 7, no. 1 (January 2007): 1–20.

———. "Portraits in Praise of a People: A Rhetorical Analysis of Norman Rockwell's Icons in Franklin D. Roosevelt's 'Four Freedoms' Campaign." *Quarterly Journal of Speech* 69, no. 1 (February 1983): 15–24.

———. "Visual Rhetoric as Indices of Political Change: A Sketch of a Conceptual, Technical Approach to Benjamin Franklin's Pictorial Representations Portraying British America." In *Visual Communication: Perception, Rhetoric, and Technology,* edited by Diane S. Hope, 177–91. Creskill, NJ: Hampton Press, 2006.

Olson, Lester C., Cara A. Finnegan, and Diane S. Hope, eds. *Visual Rhetoric: A Reader in Communication and American Culture.* Los Angeles: Sage, 2008.

Orrick, William H., Jr. *Shut It Down! A College in Crisis: San Francisco State College, October 1968–April 1969.* Washington, DC: Government Printing Office, 1969.

Ottaviani, Lorenzo. *Travel Italia: The Golden Age of Italian Travel Posters.* New York: Harry N. Abrams, 2007.

Patterson, James T. *The Eve of Destruction: How 1965 Transformed America.* New York: Basic Books, 2012.

———. *Grand Expectations: The United States, 1945–1974.* New York: Oxford University Press, 1996.

Pekar, Harvey. *Students for a Democratic Society: A Graphic History.* New York: Hill and Wang, 2008.

Perlstein, Rick. *Nixonland: The Rise of a President and the Fracturing of America*. New York: Charles Scribner's Sons, 2008.

Piquemal, Michell. *Paroles de Mai*. Paris: Albin Michel, 1998.

Poirer, Matthieu. "Hyper-optical and Kinetic Simulation, 'Happenings,' and Films in France." In *Summer of Love: Psychedelic Art, Social Crisis, and Counterculture in the 1960s*, edited by Christoph Grunenberg and Jonathan Harris, 281–302. Liverpool: Liverpool University Press, 2005.

Posters of World Wars I and II. Mineola, NY: Dover Publications, 2005.

Prelli, Lawrence J., ed. *Rhetorics of Display*. Columbia: University of South Carolina Press, 2006.

Pugliese, Stanislao G. *Desperate Inscriptions: Graffiti from the Nazi Prison in Rome, 1943–1944*. Boca Raton, FL: Bordighera, 2002.

Quigley, Tracey A. "Unheard and Unheeded: The Rhetoric of Military Dissent in the Debate over Vietnam." PhD diss., Pennsylvania State University, 2005.

Rancière, Jacques. *The Future of the Image*. Translated by Gregory Elliott. London: Verso Books, 2009.

———. *Staging the People: The Proletarian and His Double*. Translated by David Fernbach. London: Verso Books, 2011.

Raskin, Richard. *A Child at Gunpoint: A Case Study in the Life of a Photo*. Aarhus, Denmark: Aarhus University Press, 2004.

Rawls, Walton. *Wake Up, America! World War I and the American Poster*. New York: Abbeville Press, 1988.

Record, Jeffrey. *The Wrong War: Why We Lost in Vietnam*. Annapolis, MD: Naval Institute Press, 1998.

Reporting Vietnam: Part Two; American Journalism, 1969–1975. New York: Library of America, 1998.

Report of the National Advisory Commission on Civil Disorders. New York: Bantam Books, 1968.

Resnick, Elizabeth. *Design for Communication: Conceptual Graphic Design Basics*. 1st ed. Hoboken, NJ: John Wiley and Sons, 2003.

Rickards, Maurice. *Posters of Protest and Revolution*. Bath, UK: Adams and Dart, 1970.

Roberts, Helene E., ed. *Encyclopedia of Comparative Iconography: Themes Depicted in Works of Art*. 2 vols. Chicago: Fitzroy Dearborn Publishers, 1998.

Rodgers, Daniel T. *Age of Fracture*. Cambridge, MA: Harvard University Press, 2011.

Rohan, Mark. *Paris '68: Graffiti, Posters, Newspapers, and Poems of the Events of May 1968*. London: Impact Books, 1988.

Rome, Adam. *The Genius of Earth Day: How a 1970 Teach-In Unexpectedly Made the First Green Generation*. New York: Hill and Wang, 2013.

Rorabaugh, W. J. *Berkeley at War: The 1960s*. New York: Oxford University Press, 1989.

Rose, Gillian. *Visual Methodologies: An Introduction to the Interpretation of Visual Materials*. Thousand Oaks, CA: Sage, 2001.

Rosemont, Franklin, and Charles Radcliffe, eds. *Dancin' in the Streets! Anarchists, IWWs, Surrealists, Situationists, and Provos in the 1960s as Recorded in the Pages of "The Rebel Worker" and "Heatwave."* Chicago: Charles H. Kerr, 2005.

Rosenblatt, Roger. *Coming Apart: A Memoir of the Harvard Wars of 1969*. Boston: Little, Brown, 1997.

Rosenfeld, Seth. *Subversives: The FBI's War on Student Radicals, and Reagan's Rise to Power*. New York: Farrar, Straus and Giroux, 2012.

Ross, Kristin. *May '68 and Its Afterlives*. Chicago: University of Chicago Press, 2002.

Rossman, Michael. "Up Against the Wall." *Mother Jones* 18, no. 4 (July 1993): 34.

Rosteck, Thomas, ed. *At the Intersection: Cultural Studies and Rhetorical Studies*. New York: Guilford Press, 1998.

Ruth, Richard A. *In Buddha's Company: Thai Soldiers in the Vietnam War*. Honolulu: University of Hawai'i Press, 2011.

Safire, William. *Safire's New Political Dictionary: The Definitive Guide to the New Language of Politics*. New York: Random House, 1993.

Sale, Kirkpatrick. *SDS*. New York: Random House, 1973.

Sartre, Jean-Paul. *Life / Situations*. Translated by Paul Auster and Lydia Davis. New York: Pantheon, 1977.

Schlesinger, Arthur, Jr. *Violence: America in the Sixties*. New York: New American Library, 1968.

Schnapp, Jeffrey T. *Revolutionary Tides: The Art of the Political Poster, 1914–1989*. Milan: Skira, in association with the Iris and B. Gerald Cantor Center for Visual Arts at Stanford University, 2005.

Schnapp, Jeffrey T., and Matthew Tiews. *Crowds*. Stanford: Stanford University Press, 2006.

Schulz, Charles M. *The Complete Peanuts, 1950 to 1952*. Seattle, WA: Fantagraphics Books, 2004.

———. *The Complete Peanuts, 1953 to 1954*. Seattle, WA: Fantagraphics Books, 2004.

———. *The Complete Peanuts, 1967 to 1968*. Seattle, WA: Fantagraphics Books, 2008.

———. *The Complete Peanuts, 1969 to 1970*. Seattle, WA: Fantagraphics Books, 2008.

———. *Happiness Is . . . a Warm Puppy*. San Francisco: United Features Syndicate, 1979.

———. *Security Is a Thumb and a Blanket*. San Francisco: Determined Productions, 1963.

Scott, David H. T. *Poetics of the Poster: The Rhetoric of Image-Text*. Liverpool: Liverpool University Press, 2010.

Scott, Robert L., and Donald K. Smith. "The Rhetoric of Confrontation." *Quarterly Journal of Speech* 55, no. 1 (February 1969): 1–9.

Scranton, William W. *The Report of the President's Commission on Campus Unrest*. New York: Avon, 1971.

Seale, Bobby. *Seize the Time: The Black Panther Party and Huey P. Newton*. New York: Random House, 1970.

Searle, John R. *The Campus War: A Sympathetic Look at the University in Agony*. New York: World Publishing, 1971.

Seidman, Michael. *The Imaginary Revolution: Parisian Students and Workers in 1968*. New York: Berghahn Books, 2004.

Seidman, Steven A. "Barack Obama's 2008 Campaign for the U.S. Presidency and Visual Design." *Journal of Visual Literacy* 29, no. 1 (Spring 2010): 1–27.

Selz, Peter. *Art of Engagement: Visual Politics in California and Beyond*. Berkeley: University of California Press, 2005.

Selzer, Jack, and Sharon Crowley, eds. *Rhetorical Bodies*. Madison: University of Wisconsin Press, 1999.

Sharp, Gene. *The Politics of Nonviolent Action*. 3 vols. Boston: Porter Sargent, 1973.

Shawcross, William. *Sideshow: Kissinger, Nixon, and the Destruction of Cambodia*. New York: Simon and Schuster, 1979.

Sheehan, Neil. *A Bright Shining Lie: John Paul Vann and America in Vietnam*. New York: Random House, 1988.

Shepard, Leslie. *The History of Street Literature: The Story of Broadside Ballads, Chapbooks, Proclamations, News-Sheets, Election Bills, Tracts, Pamphlets, Cocks, Catchpennies, and Other Ephemera*. Detroit: Singing Tree Press, 1973.

Shikes, Ralph E. *The Indignant Eye: The Artist as Social Critic in Prints and Drawings from the Fifteenth Century to Picasso*. Boston: Beacon Press, 1976.

Sica, Alan. "Introduction: What Has 1968 Come to Mean?" In *The Disobedient Generation*, edited by Alan Sica and Stephen Turner, 1–19. Chicago: University of Chicago Press, 2005.

Sica, Alan, and Stephen P. Turner, eds. *The Disobedient Generation: Social Theorists in the Sixties*. Chicago: University of Chicago Press, 2005.

Singer, Daniel. *Prelude to Revolution: France in May 1968*. 2nd ed. Cambridge, MA: South End Press, 2002.

Situationist International. "Ten Days That Shook the University: To Create at Long Last a Situation Which Goes Beyond the Point of No Return." In *"All We Are Saying . . .": The Philosophy of the New Left*, edited by Arthur Lothstein, 82–90. New York: Capricorn, 1970.

Sixties Radicalism and Social Movement Activism: Retreat or Resurgence? New York: Anthem Press, 2010.

Skolnick, Jerome H. *The Politics of Protest*. New York: Ballantine Books, 1969.

Small, Melvin. *Antiwarriors: The Vietnam War and the Battle for America's Hearts and Minds*. Wilmington, DE: Scholarly Resources, 2002.

———. *Covering Dissent: The Media and the Anti-Vietnam War Movement*. New Brunswick: Rutgers University Press, 1994.

Small, Melvin, and William D. Hoover. *Give Peace a Chance: Exploring the Vietnam Antiwar Movement*. Syracuse: Syracuse University Press, 1992.

Solnit, Rebecca. *Secret Exhibition: Six California Artists of the Cold War Era*. San Francisco: City Lights Books, 1990.

———. *Storming the Gates of Paradise: Landscapes for Politics*. Berkeley: University of California Press, 2008.

Sontag, Susan. *On Photography*. New York: Farrar, Straus and Giroux, 1977.

Stelzner, Hermann G. "The Quest Story and Nixon's November 3, 1969 Address." *Quarterly Journal of Speech* 57, no. 2 (1971): 163–72.

Stier, Oren Baruch. Review of *A Child at Gunpoint: A Case Study in the Life of a Photo*, by Richard Raskin. *Holocaust Genocide Studies* 20, no. 2 (Fall 2006): 309–11.

Stone, Gary. *Elites for Peace: The Senate and the Vietnam War, 1964–1968*. Knoxville: University of Tennessee Press, 2007.

Sturken, Marita. "The New Aesthetics of Patriotism." *Journal of Visual Culture* 8 (2009): 168–72.

Sundell, Nina Castelli, Cleveland Center for Contemporary Art, and Lehman College Art Gallery. *The Turning Point: Art and Politics in 1968*. Cleveland, OH: Cleveland Center for Contemporary Art, 1988.

Suri, Jeremi. *The Global Revolutions of 1968: A Norton Casebook in History*. New York: W. W. Norton, 2007.

Tannenbaum, Judith, et al. *Wunderground: Providence, 1995 to the Present; Providence Poster Art*. Providence, RI: Museum of Art, 2006.

Tapies, Xavier A. *Street Art and the War on Terror: How the World's Best Graffiti Artists Said No to the Iraq War*. London: Korero Books, 2007.

Thomas, C. David, ed. *As Seen by Both Sides: American and Vietnamese Artists Look at the War*. Boston: University of Massachusetts Press, 1991.

Timmers, Margaret, ed. *The Power of the Poster*. London: V&A Publishing, 1998.

Tompkins, P. K., and E. V. B. Anderson. *Communication Crisis at Kent State: A Case Study*. New York: Gordon and Breach, 1971.

Treib, Edward Marc. "California Street Scene: Getting the Message in Berkeley." *Print* 28 (1974): 67–68.

Tulis, Jeffrey K. *The Rhetorical Presidency*. Princeton: Princeton University Press, 1987.

Turse, Nick. *Kill Anything that Moves: The Real American War in Vietnam*. New York: Henry Holt, 2013.

"Two Days in October." PBS Home Video, 2005. DVD. Produced and directed by Robert Kenner.

Unger, Irwin. *The Movement: A History of the New Left, 1959–1972*. New York: Harper and Row, 1974.

Varon, Jeremy. *Bringing the War Home: The Weather Underground, the Red Army Faction, and Revolutionary Violence in the Sixties and Seventies*. Berkeley: University of California Press, 2004.

Velonis, Anthony. *Silk Screen Technique*. New York: Creative Crafts Press, 1939.

Victoria and Albert Museum, ed. *The Power of the Poster*. London: V&A Publishing, 1998.

Von Hoffman, Nicholas. *We Are the People Our Parents Warned Us Against: A Close-up of the Whole Hippie Scene*. Greenwich, CT: Fawcett Crest, 1968.

Wagner, Ann Prentice. *1934: A New Deal for Artists*. Washington, DC: Smithsonian American Art Museum, 2009.

Walker, Daniel. *Rights in Conflict: The Violent Confrontation of Demonstrators and Police in the Parks and Streets of Chicago During the Week of the Democratic National Convention of 1968*. New York: Bantam Books, 1968.

Ward, Brian, ed. *The 1960s: A Documentary Reader*. Malden, MA: Wiley-Blackwell, 2010.

Wedgwood, C. V. *The King's Peace: 1637–1641*. New York: Macmillan, 1956.

Weschler, Lawrence. "The Graphics of Solidarity." *Virginia Quarterly Review* 82, no. 1 (Winter 2006): 111–29.

Wilentz, Sean, ed. *David Walker's Appeal in Four Articles; Together with a Preamble, to the Coloured Citizens of the World, but in Particular, and Very Expressly, to Those of the United States of America*. New York: Hill and Wang, 1995.

Wilson, Andrew. "Spontaneous Underground: An Introduction to London Psychedelic Scenes, 1965–1968." In *Summer of Love: Psychedelic Art, Social Crisis and Counterculture in the 1960s*, edited by Christoph Grunenberg and Jonathan Harris, 63–98. Liverpool: Liverpool University Press, 2005.

Wiseman, Frederick. *At Berkeley*. Cambridge, MA: Zipporah Films, 2014.

Witcover, Jules. *The Year the Dream Died: Revisiting 1968 in America*. New York: Warner Books, 1997.

Witkowski, Terrence H. "World War II Poster Campaigns: Preaching Frugality to American Consumers." *Journal of Advertising* 32, no. 1 (April 2003): 69–82.

Wolfe, Tom. *The Electric Kool-Aid Acid Test*. New York: Farrar, Straus and Giroux, 1968.

Wood, Paul, Francis Frascina, Jonathan Harris, and Charles Harrison. *Modernism in Dispute: Art Since the Forties*. New Haven: Yale University Press, 1993.

Woodeson, Alison. "'Going Back to the Land': Rhetoric and Reality in Women's Land Army Memories." *Oral History* 21, no. 2 (October 1993): 65–71.

Wortis, Joseph. *Tricky Dick and His Pals*. New York: Quadrangle / New York Times Book Co., 1974.

Yanker, Gary. *Prop Art: Over 1000 Contemporary Political Posters*. New York: Darien House, 1972.

Young, Marilyn B. *The Vietnam Wars, 1945–1990*. New York: HarperCollins, 1991.

Zaroulis, Nancy, and Gerald Sullivan. *Who Spoke Up? American Protest Against the War in Vietnam, 1963–1975*. Garden City, NY: Doubleday, 1984.

Zelizer, Barbie. *Remembering to Forget: Holocaust Memory Through the Camera's Eye*. Chicago: University of Chicago Press, 1998.

Zelko, Frank. *Make It a Green Peace! The Rise of Countercultural Environmentalism*. New York: Oxford University Press, 2013.

Zinn, Howard. *Artists in Times of War*. New York: Seven Stories Press, 2003.

INDEX

Page numbers in *italics* indicate figures.